D1374244

SWIFT'S SATIRE ON LEARNING
IN A TALE OF A TUB

69-1376

Swift's Satire
on Learning
in *A Tale of a Tub*

BY

MIRIAM KOSH STARKMAN

827.5
S977Y9

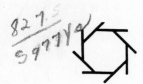

1968
OCTAGON BOOKS, INC.
New York

Alverno College Library
Milwaukee, Wisconsin

Copyright, 1950, by Princeton University Press

Reprinted 1968
by special arrangement with Princeton University Press

OCTAGON BOOKS, INC.
175 FIFTH AVENUE
NEW YORK, N. Y. 10010

LIBRARY OF CONGRESS CATALOG CARD NUMBER: 68-22296

Printed in U.S.A. by
NOBLE OFFSET PRINTERS, INC.
NEW YORK 3, N. Y.

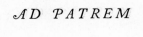
AD PATREM

PREFACE

It is difficult to express the full measure of my
indebtedness to Professor Marjorie Hope Nicolson of Columbia University, who directed the
writing of this book. Whatever is worthy in it
derives from her, her teaching, example, and
inspiration. I am also indebted to Professor
James L. Clifford of Columbia University for
his very helpful criticism of my manuscript.
President Herbert Davis of Smith College, and
Professor William Haller of Columbia University were kind enough to read my manuscript.
My friend Miss Blanche Rubinsky was my
kindly, though astute, critic through the writing
of much of this book. I should like, also, to express my appreciation to the staffs of the Columbia University Library and of the Huntington
Library in San Marino, California, for their willing and efficient aid. To the Trustees of Columbia University, who granted me a University
Fellowship which facilitated the writing of this
book, I express my gratitude. And, finally, to my
husband, Philip J. Starkman, my indebtedness
concerning this book can only be recorded, not
explained.

ACKNOWLEDGMENTS

For permission to use the copyrighted material in this volume, acknowledgment is made to the following publishers and authors: E. P. Dutton & Company, Inc., for passages from Hobbes's *Leviathan*, 1937, and Bacon's *Philosophical Works*, 1905; Appleton-Century-Crofts, Inc., for a passage from Frank Allen Patterson's *Student's Milton*, 1936; Charles Scribner's Sons, for a passage from *Descartes' Selections*, 1927; *Journal of the History of Ideas*, for passages from Philip P. Wiener's "Leibniz's Project of a Public Exhibition of Scientific Inventions," April 1940; Cambridge University Press, for passages from Sir Michael Foster's *Lectures on the History of Physiology*, 1924; Clarendon Press, for passages from Johnson's *Lives of the English Poets*, 1905, from Dryden's *Essays*, 1926, and from the Guthkelch and Nichol Smith edition of Swift's *A Tale of a Tub, Battle of the Books, and Mechanical Operation of the Spirit*, 1920; Theosophical Publishing House, for passages from Thomas Vaughan's *Works*, 1919; John Grant, Ltd., for a passage from Sir Thomas Browne's *Works*, 1912.

CONTENTS

It were much to be wisht, and I do here humbly propose for an Experiment, that every Prince in *Christendom* will take seven of the *deepest Scholars* in his Dominions, and shut them up close for *seven* Years, in *seven* Chambers, with a Command to write *seven* ample Commentaries on this comprehensive Discourse. I shall venture to affirm, that whatever Difference may be found in their several Conjectures, they will be all, without the least Distortion, manifestly deduceable from the Text.

SECTION X, *A Tale of a Tub*

INTRODUCTION

There are certain common Privileges of a Writer, the Benefit whereof, I hope, there will be no Reason to doubt; Particularly, that where I am not understood, it shall be concluded, that something very useful and profound is couch't underneath: And again, that whatever word or Sentence is Printed in a different Character, shall be judged to contain something extraordinary either of *Wit* or *Sublime.*—The Preface, *A Tale of a Tub*

POSTERITY has been pleased to accord Swift these "Privileges." It is universally agreed that *A Tale of a Tub* is a great and enduring work; but this judgment, however sound, has been based on faith, for the criticism to support it is lacking. *A Tale of a Tub* has been accepted as a series of brilliant and fortuitously arranged fragments, the digressions, tied together very loosely by a story of three brothers, Peter, Martin, and Jack, (Catholicism, Protestantism, and Nonconformity), who rent the cloaks of original Christianity left them by their father. We have Swift's word for it that his book is a satire on the "Corruptions in Religion and Learning," the tale proper carrying the satire on the abuses in religion, the digressions the satire on the abuses in learning. And the total has been construed as an erratic medley, immediate product of Swift's shattering wit, its brilliance tacitly and tactfully assumed to be an excuse for the apparent formlessness of the whole and the frequent incomprehensibility of several of its parts.

Most of the critique on *A Tale of a Tub*, from Swift's time to our own, has been devoted primarily to the religious allegory, largely to exegesis on the satire on Catholicism. It is significant, however, that Swift's satire on the "Corruptions in Religion and Learning,"[1] might more correctly read, "satire on the corruptions in learning and religion," for at least two-thirds of the book is devoted to the abuses in learning.[2] This fact was beclouded shortly after the publication of *A Tale of a Tub* in 1704, when Swift was reviled as a conscienceless enemy to religion, and his satire on the "Corruptions in Religion and Learning" was made a *cause célèbre*, as if it had been a satire on religion itself. The attack began in 1705 with William Wotton's *Observations Upon The Tale of a Tub*, in which he called the *Tale* a "crude . . . Banter upon all that is esteemed as Sacred among all Sects and Religions among Men. . . ."[3] To this Swift replied in "An Apology" added to the fifth (1710) edition of *A Tale of a Tub*:

Why should any Clergyman of our Church be angry to see the Follies of Fanaticism and Superstition exposed, tho' in the most ridiculous Manner? since that is perhaps the most probable way to cure them, or at least to hinder them from farther spreading. Besides, tho' it was not intended for their Perusal; it raillies nothing but what they preach against. It contains nothing to provoke them by the least Scurrility upon their Persons or their Functions. It celebrates the Church of England *as the most perfect of all others in Discipline and Doctrine, it advances no Opinion they reject, nor condemns any they receive.*[4]

[1] Jonathan Swift, *A Tale of a Tub to which is added The Battle of the Books and The Mechanical Operation of the Spirit*, eds., A. C. Guthkelch and D. Nichol Smith, Oxford, 1920, p. 4 (Apology).

Unless otherwise noted, all references to the *Tale* will be taken from this excellent edition.

[2] For an explanation of the apparent discrepancy between this statement and Swift's own implication that "the greatest part" of his book is the religious allegory, see Chap. 5, *infra*, especially pp. 130, 131, n.34.

This proportion of religious satire and satire on learning is also noted on p. xii of Edward Hodnett's Foreward to: Jonathan Swift, *A Tale of a Tub*, New York, Columbia University Press, 1930.

[3] William Wotton, *Defense of the Reflections upon Ancient and Modern Learning in answer to the objections of Sir W. Temple and Others. With Observations upon The Tale of a Tub*, London, 1705.

The *Observations* are reprinted in the Guthkelch-Smith edition of the *Tale* pp. 311-24. The quotation in my text is from p. 314.

[4] *A Tale of a Tub*, p. 5 (Apology).

Why should they be angry indeed? Perhaps, as Swift saw:

> . . . *the* weightiest *Men in the* weightiest *Stations are pleased to think it a more dangerous Point to laugh at those Corruptions in Religion, which they themselves must disapprove, than to endeavour pulling up those very Foundations, wherein all Christians have agreed.*[5]

That solicitude for the fair face of religion alone motivated Swift's contemporaries in their attack on *A Tale of a Tub* as irreligious and profane is doubtful. But the hue and cry was raised.[6] Swift was attacked as an enemy to religion, a subvertor of morals, an "impious Buffoon," an "Ecclesiastical *Jack Pudding*." The *Tale* was decried as "a Piece of waggish divinity, which was writ with a Design to banter all Christianity"; its profanity and "filthiness" made it "unfit for the worst of uses"; there was not "a more Blasphemous Book in our Tongue." "Not all that you and I have in the world," Smalridge told Sacheverell, "nor all that ever we shall have, should hire me to write *The Tale of a Tub*." The Duchess of Marlborough congratulated herself that Swift, who had "turned all religion into a Tale of a Tub, and sold it for a jest," had "carried his atheism and humour" to the service of the Tories. The more temperate among Swift's critics saw in *A Tale of a Tub*, if not atheism, at least an obstacle that would "prevent all friendly debate and rational remonstrance" with Anglicanism's enemies.[7] The enormous and immediate success of Swift's

[5] *Ibid.*, p. 6.

[6] See: Elsie Kligman, *Contemporary Opinion of Swift*, 1932. (An unpublished Columbia University Master's Essay.)

[7] See the following:

Sir Richard Blackmore, "Essay upon Wit," *Essays upon Several Subjects*, London, 1716, p. 217.

John Dennis, *Original Letters, Familiar, Moral and Critical*, London, 1721, II, 300.

William King, *Some Remarks on The Tale of a Tub*, in *Original Works*, London, 1776, I, 216.

Arthur Maynwaring, *Life and Posthumous Works of Arthur Maynwaring*, London, 1715, p. 201.

book must not be forgotten in the midst of all this detraction, for criticism of Swift has always been violently partisan. But the myth of *A Tale of a Tub* as an attack on religion has persisted for a long time. And pious indignation has prevented cool appraisal.

How Swift's contemporaries regarded the satire on the abuses in learning in *A Tale of a Tub* we cannot tell in any detail. Those who praised the *Tale* were general in their encomiums. Its detractors found better ammunition in the satire on the abuses in religion than in the satire on the abuses in learning. Wotton, Dennis, and Blackmore, ridiculed in *A Tale of a Tub* as exponents of Modern learning, all retaliated by attacking Swift's so-called abuse of religion. No doubt Swift's contemporaries understood the satire on the abuses in learning, topical and occasional as it is. But the keys to topical satire are easily lost in time, and the disproportionate attention devoted to Swift's satire on the corruptions in religion pushed his satire on the abuses in learning far into the background. Thus *A Tale of a Tub* was effectively broken in half, and for a long time it was read as a somewhat confusing religious allegory.

Johnson was still able to see *A Tale of a Tub* whole, and though he paid more attention to the digressions than his contemporaries, some of them saw better than he that the religious allegory was a satire on the abuses in religion rather than a satire on religion itself. But on the whole, the latter half of the eighteenth century and the first two-thirds of the nineteenth regarded *A Tale of a Tub* as a satire on religion and periodically vindicated religion against Swift's attack.

Samuel Johnson, "Swift," *Lives of the English Poets*, ed., George Birkbeck Hill, Oxford, 1905, III, 11.
Sarah, Duchess of Marlborough, *Memoirs of Sarah, Duchess of Marlborough*, ed., William King, London, 1930, p. 247.
Peter Browne, "Essay on the Characteristics," *Works of Swift* (Hawksworth ed.), London, 1775, IX, 223.

When the digressions were considered at all, they were used principally to provide proof of the dullness, diffuseness, and confusion in *A Tale of a Tub*. Not until the last third of the nineteenth century did the criticism of the *Tale* approach a clear and useful focus: the connection between *A Tale of a Tub* and the Ancients and Moderns controversy was rediscovered; and the religious allegory was found to constitute only one-third of the book.[8] That focus has not always been kept clear in our own time.

Within the last quarter of this century much of value has been written about the *Tale*. The excellent, scientific edition of *A Tale of a Tub* by A. C. Guthkelch and D. Nichol Smith in 1920 has paved the way for all students of that book. The criticism of Emile Pons is often fruitful and suggestive. Herbert Davis has indicated the right direction for the solution of many of the problems in *A Tale of a Tub*. And in the eleven pages Ricardo Quintana has devoted to a close analysis of *A Tale of a Tub* in his *Mind and Art of Jonathan Swift*, more of value was written about the *Tale* than ever before.[9] But the critical history of *A Tale of a Tub* has been a devious one, of discovery, loss, and rediscovery. While one explorer has discovered one promontory of its land, another has found a tip far removed from the first; but never have its explorers converged upon the center and found it for all time.

It is the contention of this study that within the large and comprehensive boundaries of the Ancients and Moderns controversy *A Tale of a Tub* assumes greater meaning and form than has hitherto been granted it; that Swift's work is not

---

[8] See: Donald M. Berwick, *Reputation of Jonathan Swift* (1781-1882), Philadelphia, 1941, pp. 35-37, 68-71, 105-08.

[9] Emile Pons, *Swift: Les Années de Jeunesse et le "Conte du Tonneau,"* London, 1925.

Herbert Davis, ed., *Prose Works of Jonathan Swift*, Oxford, 1939, Vol. 1 (*A Tale of a Tub*), "Introduction."

Herbert Davis, *Satire of Jonathan Swift*, New York, 1947, pp. 11-43.

Ricardo Quintana, *Mind and Art of Jonathan Swift*, New York, 1936, pp. 85-96.

only incidentally the product of a controversy between Ancients and Moderns in which Swift, like a "superman, seated far above the fray,"[10] used both sides as grist to his satiric mill; but that *A Tale of a Tub* is a self-consciously partisan document in that controversy. The connection between *A Tale of a Tub* and the battle of the books is immediately obvious and has been duly noted. Swift's predominantly Ancient temper has been recognized. But the extent to which Swift was an embattled Ancient in *A Tale of a Tub* and the degree to which the ideas in the *Tale* depend upon the whole of the Ancients and Moderns controversy, not only in letters, but more in science and philosophy, has not been appreciated.

This study is restricted to the satire on the abuses in learning in *A Tale of a Tub* and to the structure of the book insofar as it is determined by the satire on learning.[11] The religious allegory is discussed only to the extent that it determines the satire on learning. Of the two satiric themes in *A Tale of a Tub*, the satire on the abuses in religion has been studied in greater detail and to better effect; it constitutes only one-third of the book and is more obvious in its matter and method.

Nor does this study attempt to analyze the technique of Swift's irony in *A Tale of a Tub*. That is a large subject in itself[12] and one which the author is convinced should follow upon a thorough understanding of the ideas in *A Tale of a Tub*. It is certainly significant that the "Digression on Madness" displays a virtuosity of ironic techniques, which it would be interesting and valuable to explore. It seems rather more important, however, at this stage in the critical history of *A*

[10] Anne Elizabeth Burlingame, *Battle of the Books in its Historical Setting*, New York, 1920, p. 129.

See also: H. Rigault, *Histoire de la Querelle des Anciens et des Modernes*, Paris, 1856, pp. 332ff.

[11] See Chap. 5, *infra*.

[12] See: Ruby V. Redinger, "Jonathan Swift, the Disenchanter," *American Scholar*, XV, 221-26 (Spring, 1946). I understand that Dr. Redinger is engaged in a work on Swift's irony.

Tale of a Tub, that in this digression Swift satirizes, in the greatest detail, the contemporary neo-Epicurean and Hobbesian philosophies, prototypes of the new materialism, and thus arrives at his satiric characterization of that happiness which is the greatest good, as, "the sublime and refined Point of Felicity, called, *the Possession of being well deceived*; The Serene Peaceful State of being a Fool among Knaves."[13]

This study makes no pretense of being a final discovery of the *terra incognita* which is *A Tale of a Tub.* A hypothesis such as the one this study develops is not susceptible of indisputable, scientific proof. But if the collation of the intellectual milieu of Swift, the embattled moralist of Ancient persuasion, with the text *A Tale of a Tub* shows the satire to be more meaningful and formful than it has appeared to be heretofore, then the hypothesis should be of value in helping to pluck the heart of the mystery of what is indeed a very great and a very difficult book.

[13] See Chap. 2, Sect. I, *infra.*

SWIFT'S SATIRE ON LEARNING
IN A TALE OF A TUB

I

ANCIENTS AND MODERNS

RARELY has so great a book been written in a lost cause. In the war between Ancients and Moderns,[1] Swift wages a battle for the Ancients, when, for the most part, the Moderns had already effectively won that war. Swift fights a battle against the new science and philosophy when they were already powerfully entrenched. In belles-lettres, in criticism, and in education, the humanists—the Ancients—were indeed the victors for a while, though the seeds of their defeat had been firmly planted. And although there can scarcely be said to have been an Ancients *versus* Moderns controversy in religion,[2] Nonconformity was already established in England, with many of its attitudes deeply embedded in English life. Although to be Modern did not necessarily mean to believe in the idea

[1] The reader will readily see my great indebtedness, for the history of the Ancients-Moderns controversy in England, to: Richard Foster Jones, *Ancients and Moderns, A Study of the Background of the Battle of the Books*, St. Louis, Missouri, 1936. (*Washington University Studies, Language and Literature*).

See also: Richard Foster Jones, "Background of the *Battle of the Books*," *Washington University Studies*, VII, 99-162 (April, 1920).

For the history of the Ancients-Moderns controversy in France, see: Hubert Gillot, *La Querelle des Anciens et des Modernes en France*, Paris, 1914.

Rigault, *op. cit.*

[2] Since God revealed Himself when it pleased Him, there was no room for an Ancients and Moderns controversy in divinity. But according to Temple, the Ancient fathers were greater than Modern clergymen, just as Hippocrates was greater than any contemporary physician, and Archimedes greater than any contemporary mathematician. See: Sir William Temple, *Some Thoughts Upon Reviewing the Essay of Ancient and Modern Learning*, in *Works*, London, 1814, III, 509ff. (Hereafter this essay will be referred to as *Some Thoughts Upon Reviewing the Essay*.)

of Progress, to be Ancient was necessarily to be militantly opposed to that idea.[3] And *A Tale of a Tub* is one of the greatest satires on progress ever written, though the idea of Progress as we now know it was still in its youth at the time Swift wrote *A Tale of a Tub*. And here, perhaps, lies the critical dilemma in *A Tale of a Tub*. To conceive of Swift as an enemy to progress, when we are the heirs of that very progress that Swift would have exterminated in the seed, interferes seriously with the cult of the writer as hero. Standing at the crossroads between the old learning and the new, Swift rejected and reviled the new learning, fully conscious of all the issues, and militant before the Lord. *A Tale of a Tub* is the expression of Swift's deep-seated and consistent conservatism, from which bias he looked at every facet of life and found the old better than the new. What bred this cast of mind is not a question to be answered lightly, nor is it very significant to our purposes here. The fact is that this was his point of view at the time he wrote *A Tale of a Tub*. And it is significant, too, that although Swift was to become more flexible towards Modernity later, by and large, and with only minor changes, at the time he wrote *A Tale of a Tub* he had achieved full intellectual maturity, and little was to be added to the sum of his ideas; just as little was to be added to the sum of Milton's ideas after he had reached the age of twenty-five. It may, indeed, be argued that in *A Tale of a Tub* Swift achieved a greater intellectual stature than he was ever to achieve again.

Exactly when Swift wrote *A Tale of a Tub* cannot be determined definitely. The most persuasive answer to the question still rests upon the evidence of Swift's own words in the "Apology": "*The greatest Part of that Book was finished above thirteen Years since, 1696, which is eight Years before it was published.*" It is to be remembered, however, that although

[3] See: J. B. Bury, *Idea of Progress*, London, 1920, *passim*.

all reports about a very early inception of the work (1686) are unsubstantiated, Swift assures us that his *"Discourse is the Product of the Study, the Observation, and the Invention of several Years. . . ."* "The greatest part" must refer principally to the religious allegory; from such slender evidence as we have, we may conclude that large parts of the digressions (especially those referring to the Phalaris Controversy, from which, as we shall see, a great deal of Swift's satire stems) could not have been written earlier than late 1697. We know the dedication to Lord Somers and the "Bookseller to the Reader" were written between 1702 and 1704. Undoubtedly minor revisions and additions were made up to the date of publication.[4]

What then was it to be an Ancient in the 1690's?

The answer lies in all the shifting complexities of the Ancients-Moderns controversy. It is not our purpose to explain that controversy; that has already been done excellently. But those facts of the controversy which are crucial to the understanding of *A Tale of a Tub*, and many of them are, must be recognized. Primarily the war between Ancients and Moderns was being fought in France and England, though the individual battles were somewhat differently directed in each country. It appears that Swift's approach to the controversy was primarily native, though undoubtedly some facets of the French controversy influenced him. But the results were the same. It is true that in each country the controversy was independently pursued, but the French and English both were fighting for the same goals.

French modernism was primarily Cartesian, philosophical, and interested in pure science. English modernism was Baconian, experimental, and utilitarian. The English controversy was devoted principally to the experimental philosophy;

---

[4] Davis, ed., *A Tale of a Tub*, "Introduction."
Guthkelch-Smith, *op. cit.*, pp. xl-xliv.

the French gave fuller expression to the literary phase of the controversy. Thus criticism of Homer, or anti-Homerism as it may be called, is to be found more fully expressed in France,[5] but there was much of it in England. The virtuoso-projector as a type is natively English, although there was much French satire of the new scientists. Again, although Jansenism in many ways affected France as Puritanism did England, there is no doubt that Jack is native Englishman to the bone. Although the idea of Progress was evolved primarily in France, all the concepts and attitudes leading to the formulation of that idea were simultaneously entertained in England, either as independent developments or as importations. Certainly the English, like the French, were committed to the same optimistic and rationalistic temper of mind that broke with the authority of the Ancients, that rejected the theory of degeneration, that believed that the business of science was the "benefit of man's estate," that now saw the laws of the universe as constant and immutable, and that had faith in science to unriddle those constant and unchanging laws. We shall, then, look for the historical backgrounds of *A Tale of a Tub* where we find them, but the fact remains that we find them primarily in England.[6]

First, it is important to determine why in his satire on Modernity Swift joined the two streams of religion and learning. Religion and learning were by no means the discrete realms in the seventeenth century that they are now. Even

[5] See the following:
  Rigault, *op. cit., passim.*
  Gillot, *op. cit., passim.*
  Bury, *op. cit.,* pp. 79-81.
[6] Jones's thesis in *Ancients and Moderns*, that the root of the quarrel which culminated in Swift's *Battle of the Books* lay in England rather than France, a quarrel principally between the upholders of the new against the old learning, rather than a product of a French literary quarrel, is now beyond dispute; and the thesis holds for the *Tale* as much as, if not more than, for the *Battle*. Nevertheless, I do not find the divorce between the French and English Ancients-Moderns controversies as complete as does Jones.

more intrinsically connected were what were considered abuses
in religion and learning. Enthusiasm in religion, it was commonly believed, begot enthusiasm in learning. The new
learning was suspected of atheism, even as Nonconformity
was feared as potentially subversive of all religion. But more
immediately, both were accused of extremism. The new learning never completely lost its Puritan stigma in the seventeenth
century; and with very little reason, both the new learning
and Nonconformity were sometimes suspected of devious
affiliations with Catholicism.[7] Hence the connection between
the digressions in *A Tale of a Tub* and Peter and Jack, with
Martin providing the satiric norm. In joining the satire on
the abuses in religion and learning in one book, then, Swift
was merely taking the whole contemporary intellectual milieu
as his target and ascribing one and the same error to all its
parts—Modernity.

The inevitable alignment of the old and the new, the effort
of the new to establish itself, of the old to retain its vested
interests, expressed itself in the seventeenth century by this
question, "Which is better, the old learning or the new?"
If the new, the authority of the old must be broken and the
new established. Or as the combatants in the Ancients-Mod-

---

[7] For the connections between the new learning and Catholicism, see
Chap. 3, *infra.*

The suspicion of a united front between Catholics and Nonconformists
was fairly pervasive. Although the Catholics came in for privileges intended for the Nonconformists in Charles II's Act of Indulgence, and the
Nonconformists were relieved by the Declaration of Indulgence of King
James, who intended relief only for the Catholics, Catholics and Nonconformists scarcely presented a united front against Establishment. See: J.
R. Green, *Short History of the English People*, New York, 1876, II, 649,
650.

The Catholics, however, apparently made overtures to the Nonconform-
ists. See, for example: W. H., *Puritan Convert*, London, 1676. In this tract a
Catholic priest, who calls himself a "Prelatickal Protestant," woos the
Nonconformist, on the grounds that both are opposed to Establishment,
and, more curiously, because Nonconformity is only a step on the way to
Catholicism.

erns controversy asked the question more specifically, which had the greater genius and learning, Antiquity or Modernity? And when the question was asked so specifically, some of the most ardent Moderns in England were reluctant to break with their cultural heritage completely, and they were willing to concede that Antiquity had had the greater genius, although Modernity had the greater learning, a concession, incidentally, which did not interfere seriously with their Modern efforts.

The earliest comprehensive idea of the Moderns was a negative one—the rejection of the Theory of Nature's Decay,[8] or as it was known earlier, the Theory of Degeneration; a theory that was as old as the concept of the Golden Age; a theory that was to re-assert itself, with modifications, in Europe as late as 1918 with Spengler. This theory, with its accumulation of subordinations and variations, left its indelible mark on *A Tale of a Tub*, for inherent in the rejection of the Theory of Degeneration lies, potentially, the espousal of the idea of Progress. If nature, and therefore man, does not decay, and each age provides its increment of progress, we may look forward to an almost infinite, utopian progress, to a posterity always greater than the however-great present. That increment of progress was guaranteed by Descartes, by the hypothesis that the order of the universe remains constant, and the belief that science, a kind of evolutionary method in which one branch grows from the maturity of the other, can decipher that order, at least up to that indefinite point when all the riddles shall have been deciphered. That this idea of Progress was sharply in conflict with the orthodox

---

[8] Note that although Swift rejected the idea of Progress, he did not necessarily subscribe to the Theory of Nature's Decay. Note his satirical " '. . . *we live in the very Dregs of Time,*' " *Tale of a Tub*, p. 52 (Preface). In *Gulliver* (II, 7) he doubted the grounds of quarreling with Nature. See: Jonathan Swift, *Gulliver's Travels*, in *Prose Works of Jonathan Swift*, ed., Herbert Davis, Oxford, 1941, 121ff. Swift's dislike for the Theory of Nature's Decay may well have stemmed from his distaste for Puritan jeremiads on the evils of the times.

idea of Providence, that keeps God free, unbound by immutable laws, to alter His universe, that allows for millennia only by divine intervention, is clear. And it is equally clear that Swift, like many others, understood the conflict between these two ideas and rejected Progress for Providence, Swift who could not ignore the conflict and would not turn the God of his fathers into a Prime Mover.

Furthermore, Swift as moralist found it hard to reconcile the faith in Progress with the shortcomings of the world around him, so sharply defined by the recorded magnificence of the past. It is from the Moderns' rejection of the Theory of Nature's Decay, from his own Ancient and orthodox rejection of Progress, that Swift derives his prime and pervasive satiric rule in *A Tale of a Tub,* the mock assumption that last is best, and the later will be even better.

But I here think fit to lay hold on that great and honourable Privilege of being the *Last Writer;* I claim an absolute Authority in Right, as the *freshest Modern,* which gives me a Despotick Power over all Authors before me.[9]

With extraordinary clarity, Swift sees the chief implications of the idea of Progress, and especially the need for steady reference to the past and future. He treats time bi-dimensionally, as if it were laid out flat upon the table of history like a sheet of paper. Back and forth his pen moves remorselessly, collating here, subtracting there, and with the most devastating ease he finds that the facts of history do not prove the theory of Progress.[10]

Another important idea of the Moderns, an idea essential to the theory of Progress, is the idea of utility, the usefulness of knowledge, the *finis scientiarum.* This was Bacon's great contribution. His pervasive utilitarianism provided the impetus for experimentation, and implied the nearly complete

[9] *A Tale of a Tub,* p. 130 (Digression in the Modern Kind).
[10] See especially "The Epistle Dedicatory to His Royal Highness, Prince Posterity."

rejection of authority, and the relegation of God to an uncontroversial position, for in religion he found "no deficience." He provided, in short, the technique and morality of Modernity. Swift never satirizes Bacon, preferring Descartes as his target; he is, nevertheless, merciless to Baconianism and even more merciless to pseudo-Baconianism. For, indeed, there were many who either mistook the emphases and the goals of the master, or prostituted his ideas. The quick and easy learners, the useless systematizers, the over-hasty concluders, all are targets for Swift's satire in *A Tale of a Tub*.[11] Justifiably or not, they were, in the eyes of the beholder, Moderns.

The utilitarian ideal was to be emphasized by the Puritans far more than Lord Verulam ever intended. The Puritans left other stigmas on Modernism too. Humanistic learning was by its very nature an aristocratic pursuit; learning among many and the most notorious of the sectarians was democratized to a degree alarming to the conservatives. Bacon had emphasized the need for humble workers in the vineyards of the new learning; the Nonconformists suffered them, willingly, to be as plebeian as their mechanick preachers. The utilitarianism of the Nonconformists ran rampant, a utilitarianism that soon grew utopian in its vision. "The common good," "the benefit of man's estate," "the public good" were emphasized endlessly as the Nonconformists saw that Baconianism was neatly consonant with their own reforming temper, with godliness, democracy, and good business.[12] Often their utopia of progress was not even relegated to the era of Prince Posterity but appeared to be right at hand in England's green and pleasant land. Swift looked for evidences

[11] See Chap. 3, *infra*.

[12] ". . . Modern scientific utilitarianism is the offspring of Bacon begot upon Puritanism." (Jones, *Ancients and Moderns*, p. 92.)

See also: Robert K. Merton, "Puritanism, Pietism, and Science," *Sociological Review*, XXVIII, 1-30 (Jan., 1936).

of the utopia of progress about him, but found instead only madness and depravity.[13]

Cartesianism, providing the last important link to forge the chain of progress, the faith in the invariability of the laws of nature and the power of science to explain those laws, was perhaps the chief fly in the honey pot of Modernism; a fly even the most faithful of the Moderns felt obliged to swat regularly. Many of the most influential of the Moderns in England and France were busy keeping their skirts clear of Descartes. Pascal rejected him, Malebranche grew suspect by apologizing for him, Sprat repulsed him, Glanvil questioned him, and Wotton evaded him.[14] Though the Royal Society might well have called him master far more than Bacon, officially it would accept him only as a hypothesis.

I do not here reckon the several *Hypotheses* of *Des-Cartes, Gassendi,* or *Hobbes,* as Acquisitions to real Knowledge, since they may only be Chimaera's and amusing Notions, fit to entertain working Heads. I only alledge such Doctrines as are raised upon faithful Experiments, and nice Observations; and such Consequences as are the immediate Results of, and manifest Corollaries drawn from, these Experiments and Observations: Which is what is commonly meant by *Theories.*[15]

And indeed they needed to be nervous and careful, for every time the New Science was impugned as atheistical the suspicion of Cartesianism lay at the root. Dualism or no, Descartes gave a purely mechanical interpretation of the universe, with God, at best, a deistical Prime Mover. Swift too took cognizance of Descartes—as one of the prototypes of the mad

[13] See Chap. 2, *infra.*
[14] Jones, *Ancients and Moderns,* pp. 239-40.
  Louis I. Bredvold, "Dryden, Hobbes, and the Royal Society," *Modern Philology,* xxv, 425-31 (May, 1928).
[15] William Wotton, *Reflections Upon Ancient and Modern Learning,* London, 1694, p. 244. (Unless otherwise noted, the first edition of the *Reflections* is used throughout this study.)

Modern philosopher, of the mad philosophical state, of the "Digression on Madness."[16]

With the Restoration and the growth of the Royal Society came the widespread discipline to the doctrines of Modernity, a discipline which, in addition to its doctrine, provided Swift with some of his sharpest barbs against Modernity, against the virtuoso-projector in his milieu.[17]

These, then, are some of the basic issues of the Ancients and Moderns controversy, as they are reflected in *A Tale of a Tub,* up to the time in 1690 when Sir William Temple called wrath down upon his unsuspecting head by engaging in a gentlemanly exercise, *An Essay upon the Ancient and Modern Learning,*[18] in which, incidentally, he cited the spurious Phalaris letters as a detail in proof of Ancient superiority. When Temple revived the Ancients-Moderns controversy, he was for all practical purposes summoning a ghost, however unquietly laid; nor did he suspect the old ghost had so much blood in it. In addition to reviving the theory of the controversy, he was to begin a pamphlet war in which Swift, as apologist for his patron, was to write a monumental work of universal proportions, and at the same time to use all the weapons of diatribe, innuendo, and parody germane to the most immediately partisan pamphlet. This to a considerable extent complicates our problem of understanding *A Tale of a Tub,* for, before the satire will emerge clearly, we must reckon with its immediate, occasional character as well as with its philosophical and theoretical character. Much of the satire in *A Tale of a Tub* is universal in the best sense of that word; much of it is purely occasional. That is, in *A Tale of a Tub* Swift is battling not only Modernity, not only

[16] See Chap. 2, Sect. 1, *infra.*
[17] See Chap. 3, *infra.*
[18] See: Sir William Temple, *Essay Upon the Ancient and Modern Learning,* in *Works,* London, 1814, III, 444-86. (Hereafter referred to as *Essay* in this study.)

Bentley and Wotton as Moderns, but Bentley and Wotton, two presumptuous critics of Sir William Temple.

Actually, since all the decisive arguments of the Moderns had already been made by the last quarter of the seventeenth century, all that remained for the Ancient of faith was to recapitulate what had been said before, and to pit more great Ancient names and deeds against more Modern names and deeds, to the credit of Antiquity. But it is easier to insist upon the greatness of an Ancient than of a Modern. It may be said that the defenders of the Ancients in the seventeenth century always had an easier time of it than the defenders of the Moderns, and they frequently labored under the delusion that they were the victors even in the midst of their most abysmal rout; for every fresh innovation required another attack on authority, and the burden of the proof lay on the shoulders of the Moderns. Thus Temple casually reviews the superior virtues of Antiquity, and in his rejection of natural philosophy badly underestimates even the Harveys and Descartes's of Modernity.

To what extent Temple's scepticism of natural philosophy strengthened Swift's youthful dislike for the subject is conjectural. It is more significant that Temple's espousal of the Ancient cause was made neither so much in the name of science nor of letters as in the name of moral philosophy.[19] His moralistic temper provides a more important link between Temple and *A Tale of a Tub* than any specific details we find in the *Essay upon the Ancient and Modern Learning*. Many details, however, are common both to the *Essay* and to *A Tale of a Tub*, and undoubtedly the *Essay* recalled to Swift some of the chief issues of the Ancients-Moderns controversy. The

[19] See the following:

Clara Marburg, *Sir William Temple, A Seventeenth Century "Libertin,"* New Haven, 1932.

Homer E. Woodbridge, *Sir William Temple, The Man and his Work,* New York, 1940, Chap. XXIII.

genius versus learning argument is here. The dwarf-giant image is recalled;[20] and although Swift does not use the figure itself, the concept of Prince Posterity, the all-knowing youth in his nonage, may well have had his origins in the *Essay*:

A boy of fifteen is wiser than his father at forty, the meanest subject than his Prince or Governors; and the modern scholars, because they have, for a hundred years past, learned their lesson pretty well, are much more knowing than the ancients their masters.[21]

The end of Temple's *Essay* is clearly reflected in *A Tale of a Tub*: Temple's analysis of the decay of learning since the Renaissance as it was caused by dissension in religion,[22] and by the "satyrical itch" which in its "scorn of pedantry" eventually resulted in the scorn of learning.[23] But most significant to our purposes is Temple's rejection of the theory of Progress in his *Essay upon the Ancient and Modern Learning*. His substitution for the theory of Progress of his own cyclical theory of civilization, a process of alternate decay and regeneration, is more important in itself than to our understanding of *A Tale of a Tub*; but his complete rejection of Progress is mirrored in Swift's basic attitude towards Modernity throughout *A Tale of a Tub*.

[20] The dwarf-giant image, the Moderns being the dwarfs, the Ancients the giants, persisted throughout the Ancients-Moderns controversy. (Jones, *Ancients and Moderns*, p. 293, n. 12.)
Some of the dwarfs found themselves the taller for being seated on the shoulders of the giants, but Temple refused to grant them this eminence of place: ". . . if we are dwarfs we are still so though we stand upon a giant's shoulders; and even so placed, yet we see less than he, if we are naturally shorter sighted, or if we do not look as much about us, or if we are dazzled with the height, which often happens from weakness either of heart or brain." (Temple, *Essay*, p. 462.)

[21] Temple, *Essay*, p. 476.

[22] Note that Wotton disputes this point with Temple, in a very tentative way: "Yet, considering all things, it may be justly questioned, whether Learning may not by these very Disputes [in religion], have received either immediately, or occasionally, a very great Improvement, or at least, suffered no very considerable Diminutions." (Wotton, *Reflections*, p. 343.)

[23] Compare *A Tale of a Tub*, pp. 48ff. (Preface) with Temple, *Essay*, pp. 484ff. See also Chap. 4, *infra*.

Temple clearly saw the implications of the Ancients-Moderns controversy, and he was deeply aware of the extent to which a Modern victory imperilled the *status quo*.

. . . our different opinions in religion and the factions they have raised or animated for fifty years past, have had an ill effect upon our manners and customs, inducing more avarice, ambition, disguise (with the usual consequences of them) than were ever before in our constitution. From all this may happen, that there is no where more true zeal in the many different forms of devotion and yet no where more knavery under the shows and pretences. There are no where so many disputers upon religion, so many reasoners upon government, so many refiners in politics, so many curious inquisitives, so many pretenders to business and state-employments, greater porers upon books, nor plodders after wealth; and yet no where more abandoned libertines, more refined luxurists, extravagant debauchees, conceited gallants, more dabblers in poetry as well as politics, in philosophy, and in chemistry. I have had several servants far gone in divinity, others in poetry; have known, in the families of some friends, a keeper deep in the Rosycrucian principles, and a laundress firm in those of Epicurus.[24]

This is essentially the same ground that Swift covers in *A Tale of a Tub*. The revolt in religion has broken the golden chain; religion and learning have become vulgarized; the mechanick sets up his own religious state; the witling his philosophy, science, aesthetic, and political state; and each would establish his own doctrine and discipline. Or, in *A Tale of a Tub* Catholicism and Nonconformity are rebuked, and the new science, philosophy, and critique are all brought up to the mirror of tried and established thought and found wanting and perverse.

When William Wotton entered the breach[25] in 1694 with

---

[24] Sir William Temple, *Of Poetry*, in *Works*, London, 1814, III, 440.
    Note also the similarity of the quoted passage to: "It is the disease of the times, reigning in all places. New Sects: new religions: new philosophie: new methods: all new, till all be lost." (Meric Casaubon, *Treatise Concerning Enthusiasme*, London, 1656, p. 185.)
[25] For an excellent bibliography of the Phalaris Controversy, see: A.

his reply to Temple's *Essay*, the *Reflections Upon Ancient and Modern Learning*, he fought the good fight for Modernity in reasonable and accepted terms, and distinguished himself by the thoroughness and justness of his analysis. Although Swift engaged in a good deal of personal diatribe against him, Wotton's ideas were perfectly orthodox. He respectfully repudiated authority when it disputed reason, and nobly defended the new learning. But what is most significant to our purposes here is Wotton's faith in the prog-

---

Guthkelch, ed., *Battle of the Books by Jonathan Swift; with Selections from the Literature of the Phalaris Controversy*, London, 1908.

The following list of items pertinent to our purposes here is excerpted from Guthkelch's bibliography (pp. 297-305) for the convenience of the reader, since my own citations of these works do not always refer to the original editions.

  a) *Miscellanea*. The Second Part. In Four Essays, By Sir William Temple . . . The Second Edition*. . . London, 1690.
      I.   Upon Ancient and Modern Learning
      II. Upon the Gardens of Epicurus
      III. Upon Heroick Vertue
      IV. Upon Poetry
      [*This so-called second edition is the earliest edition extant.]
  b) *Reflections Upon Ancient and Modern Learning*. By William Wotton . . . 1694.
  c) Φαλαριδος Ακραγαητιηωη Τυραηηοι Επιστολαι
      Phalaridis Agrigentinorum Tyranni Epistolae
      Car. Boyle, . . . 1695.
  d) *Reflections upon Ancient and Modern Learning*. By William Wotton. . . The Second Edition with large Additions.* *With a Dissertation upon the Epistles of Phalaris, Themistocles, Socrates, Euripides, etc. and Aesop's Fables.* By Dr. Bentley. . . 1697.
      [*The "large additions" are, in effect, very small. They consist of a short section on surgery, and one on agriculture and gardening. The rest remains the same as in the first edition.]
  e) *Dr. Bentley's Dissertations on the Epistles of Phalaris and the Fables of Aesop*, Examin'd by the Honourable Charles Boyle . . . 1698.
  f) *A Dissertation upon the Epistles of Phalaris*. With An Answer to the Objections of the Honourable Charles Boyle. . . By Richard Bentley. . . 1699.
  g) *Dialogues of the Dead*. Relating to the present Controversy concerning the Epistles of Phalaris. By the Author of the Journey to London. . . 1699. [William King]
  h) *A Short Review of the Controversy between Mr. Boyle and Dr. Bentley*. . . 1701. [Francis Atterbury]

ress of his own age, especially in natural science, which he suspected was all but complete.

From all which [scientific societies] such Swarms of Great men in every Part of Natural and Mathematical Knowledge have within these few Years appeared, that it may, perhaps, without Vanity, be believed, that if this Humour lasts much longer, and learned men do not divert their Thoughts to Speculations of another Kind, the next Age will not find very much Work of this Kind to do.[26]

He exhibited a typical Christian nervousness as he confronted his faith in the new learning with his beliefs in the imperfections of mankind, but that nervousness was easily pushed to the background. He had the exhilaration of a man living in a golden age of learning and he felt that, in mathematics, physiology, and natural history, at least, the millennium had all but come. It is this pride and millenarian enthusiasm that evoked some of Swift's sharpest satire: ". . . it is reckoned, that there is not at this present, a sufficient quantity of New Matter left in Nature, to furnish and adorn any one particular Subject to the Extent of a Volume."[27]

Boyle's edition of the Phalaris epistles in 1695 marks the beginnings of a minor engagement, the Phalaris controversy, stemming from, though tangential to, the main issue of the Ancients-Moderns controversy, the superiority of the Ancient over the Modern learning. Although Boyle defends Temple's claim for the authenticity of the Phalaris letters in his preface,[28] he is not interested at the moment in the Ancients-Moderns controversy. Wotton's second edition of his *Reflec-*

[26] Wotton, *op. cit.*, p. 348.

Note, however, that Wotton does not subscribe to indefinite Progress. In the "Preface" to the *Reflections* he says he writes to dispute the "*Eternity of the World*" idea, which is anti-Christian. He writes merely to show "that the World has improved" and that "it is at present much more knowing than it ever was since the earliest Times to which History can carry us."

[27] *A Tale of a Tub*, p. 146 (Digression in Praise of Digressions).

[28] Charles Boyle, Φαλαριδος Ακραγαητιηωη Τυραηοι Επιστολαι, Oxford, 1718, Preface.

tions, in 1697, substantially the same as the first, is less important in itself than as the occasion of Richard Bentley's first *Dissertation upon the Epistles of Phalaris, Themistocles, Socrates, Euripides* which was appended to it. And Bentley's first *Dissertation*, an examination of the Phalaris epistles on sixteen counts proving them spurious, is less significant than his second *Dissertation* in 1699. Between these two dissertations came the rebuttal to the first. *Dr. Bentley's Dissertations on the Epistles of Phalaris, and the Fables of Aesop,* "Examined by the Honourable Charles Boyle," in 1698, Boyle's in name, but authored largely by several of the Christ Church Wits, Smalridge, Freind, Atterbury, and Alsop. In this witty piece, which took the town, the focus of attention is on the Ancients-Moderns controversy, and the problem of the authenticity of Phalaris is relegated to the background.[29] To this Bentley replied in his second *Dissertation*, a reprint of the sixteen sections of his original *Dissertation*, each followed by a long and elaborate defense of his point, of which the immense classical erudition has since become famous; and, in addition, a reply to the personal as well as the academic objections, of which there were many, of his "Examiners."[30] With William King's *Dialogues of the Dead* in 1699, the bridge between the Phalaris dispute and *A Tale of a Tub* was complete, for King used satire exclusively to dismay the Bentley-Wotton faction, and many of his satirical details bear marked resemblance to *A Tale of a Tub*.[31] With Francis Atterbury's *Short Review of the Controversy between Mr. Boyle and Dr. Bentley*, in 1701, this latest skirmish in the Ancients-

[29] Charles Boyle, *Dr. Bentley's Dissertations on the Epistles of Phalaris, and the Fables of Aesop, Examin'd*, London, 1698.

[30] Richard Bentley, *Works of Richard Bentley*, ed., Alexander Dyce, London, 1836, 3 vols. (Vols. I and part of II are devoted to the *Dissertations* as it appeared in its second and enlarged edition.)

[31] See Chap. 3, *infra*, for connections between the *Tale* and the *Dialogues*.
William King, *Dialogues of the Dead, Relating to the present Controversy Concerning the Epistles of Phalaris*, in *Original Works of William King*, London, 1776, I, 133-86.

Moderns controversy left its Phalaris tangent and swung back to the original point where it began, with Temple's *Essay upon the Ancient and Modern Learning*, for Atterbury made it plain that he was interested not so much in the validity of Phalaris as in what constitutes proper learning.[32] And all this elaborate pamphlet war is to be found reflected in *A Tale of a Tub*, especially in Swift's satire on Modern criticism, in the "Digression concerning Criticks."[33]

These, however, are the bare bones of history. We may ask ourselves again what it was to be Ancient in the 1690's. It was to be one, or several, of very different persuasions on many different levels and tangents. It was perhaps to be a gentleman, product of an aristocratic education, in distinction to being bourgeois or a mechanick, whether a mechanick in science, religion, or letters. It was perhaps to be a gentleman objecting to a Bentley, just as gently educated as oneself, a Bentley confuting a nobleman if only on the subject of Phalaris, about which he knew more than Boyle and Temple together. One might be an Ancient because one preferred classical to Modern literature and thought it preposterous for a Perrault to find fault with Homer.

One might easily dislike sectarians as opposed to Establishment in the seventeenth century and be an Ancient, although one might be a Modern and share that dislike. But one might suspect the atheistic, know the Enthusiastic, and imagine the Catholic affiliations of the new learning, and especially if one be an orthodox churchman, reject Modernity. Even if one were Robert Boyle, one might feel the need to protest one's religious orthodoxy.[34] The consistent Ancient felt no such need.

[32] Francis Atterbury, *Short Review of the Controversy between Mr. Boyle, and Dr. Bentley*, London, 1701, pp. 4ff.

[33] See Chap. 4, *infra*.

[34] See: Robert Boyle, *The Christian Virtuoso: Shewing That by being addicted to Experimental Philosophy, a Man is rather Assisted, than Indisposed, to be a Good Christian*, London, 1690.

In the realm of philosophy, an Ancient need not be an Aristotelian, but he could certainly not be a Cartesian. One could be an Ancient and simultaneously attack Epicureanism in the late seventeenth century, for the simple reason that Epicurus had become Modern.[35]

To be an Ancient in the seventeenth century one need have had no great quarrel with Bacon, but one could speak as a "man of business," from one's social conscience, and question the propriety and utility of Modern science. One could speak as a man of Reason against the horde of fanatic quacks, parasites upon Baconianism. One could, if one were well versed in tried and established humanistic learning, and especially if one had the temper of a moralist and the gifts of a satirist, easily differentiate between the sound and the spurious in Antiquity, and easily confuse the Modern parasite with his host, all to the further discredit of Modernity. To see Swift as an Ancient in *A Tale of a Tub* is to see him in all these ramifications of that persuasion.

The completeness of the design of *A Tale of a Tub,* as it took all knowledge to be its province, is broken in one major respect, but it is a break that by no means disturbs our thesis. There is no battle of the books in *A Tale of a Tub,* except in a few minor details, no argument whether the Ancients or the Moderns were greater in belles-lettres. That argument is expounded in Swift's *Battle of the Books,* a discrete work, but one which was written simultaneously with the digressions in the *Tale,* and which is, as it were, a chapter of that book. To see *A Tale of a Tub* whole is to read the *Battle of the Books* neither before nor after it, but somewhere along the middle, as if the *Battle* were labeled, "A Digression giving a Full and True Account of the Battel Fought last Friday Between the Antient and the Modern Books in St. James's Library." The fact that Swift wrote the *Battle of the Books* as a separate

[35] See Chap. 2, Sect. 1, *infra.*

work left him the province of criticism, or the learning of literature rather than its art, to be explored in *A Tale of a Tub*. In fragments, by indirection, emerges Swift's critical faith, Ancient and consistently neoclassical.[36]

Well entrenched, militant, and excited as the New Science was in the late seventeenth century, it was most vulnerable to the satirist of Ancient persuasion. It was simultaneously result of and support for the new materialistic philosophy. Together they threatened to rock orthodox Christianity. Whether the New Philosophy were materialistic or mechanistic, whether it were Baconian, Cartesian, Hobbesian, or neo-Epicurean, whether it explained matter as atomic or corpuscular, it was justifiably suspected of its logical conclusions—atheism. Together the contemporary science and philosophy had affiliations, real or imagined, with Enthusiasm, Popery, and Dissent. They were both easily confused with occultism, whether practical or philosophical.[37] And whether bright or dark, speculative philosophy was for Swift always uncomfortably suspect of an obscurantism that confused the simple, fundamental truths of Christianity. Herein lay the basis of his anti-intellectualism, an anti-intellectualism that was enhanced by his moralistic temper, and was determined by the necessarily negative approach of the satirist. Swift's contemporaries vaguely understood that anti-intellectualism when they deplored his satire on the abuses of religion in *A Tale of a Tub*; for although Swift says his book *"Celebrates the Church of England as the most perfect of all others in Discipline and Doctrine,"*[38] he speaks loosely: the praise emerges faintly and only by indirection. Actually his purpose was not to praise Establishment as it flourished in England in his time. Considerably less was he willing to uphold the peripatetic philosophy and science. He was interested in subvert-

[36] See Chap. 4, *infra.*
[37] See Chap. 2, Sect. II, *infra.*
[38] *A Tale of a Tub*, p. 5 (Apology).

ing Modernity. Hence he ridiculed the New Science as vain in its aims, ludicrous in its methods, besotted in its personnel, and a-social in its results. To the pedant-plebeian, prototype of the Modern critics, is added another ingredient, and the scientist in *A Tale of a Tub* emerges as the pedant-plebeian-fool. Swift's philosopher is primarily the madman, just as his Nonconformist Jack is the madman. All the Moderns in *A Tale of a Tub* have a goodly quantity of knavery, and especially Catholic Peter. Taken together, this is Modernity, the abuses in religion and learning, the departure from the sane, orderly, established way of life, the sad state of England. This, says Swift, is the Moderns' pride, their Progress.

Thus it was to be Ancient in respect to learning and religion in the late seventeenth century, when Swift wrote his *Tale*. And right or wrong, the position was nevertheless consistent and meaningful, especially to a satirist and moralist. The learning of the Ancients was several thousand years old, and its details and machinery meaningful in the light of the whole. The learning of the Moderns was still in its cradle; much of it was misguided; much amorphous; much of it was devoted to the development of a terminology and a method; much of it has achieved meaning only in subsequent history; some of it has not achieved meaning yet. And if that learning seemed to go hand in hand with nonconformity, and the apparent excesses of each seemed to support and lead the other along the path of darkness, one rejected both, and affiliated oneself with Antiquity. Hence Swift's rejection of Modernity in *A Tale of a Tub*.

2

PHILOSOPHY, OLD AND NEW,
BRIGHT AND DARK

God make me constant to that profession of *Tertullian* . . . .
There is no need of curiosity (after Oracles, or Prophets, or Philosophers, to teach the way to happinesse) *after Christ Jesus: nor
of inquisition, after his Gospel. When we professe our selves to
believe* (being well grounded by good Catechizing, etc. in the
Christian faith,) *all our desires, and all our endeavours in point of
believing are at end.*

Neither do I think we need to seek the *Image of God* in man elsewhere, then in perfect Reason; such as he was created in.

Casaubon, *Treatise Concerning Enthusiasme*[1]

SWIFT was a satirist because he was a moralist; he was a moralist because he was a Christian; and because he was so earnest
a Christian, he was a pessimist. And to the moralist, pessimist,
and satirist, speculative philosophy held little charm. The
realm of *A Tale of a Tub* is not the nature of man in the
universe, but the behavior of man in the world. Swift's purpose was to persuade man to virtue and to dissuade him from
vice. To achieve virtue man needs the simple truths of Christianity, not the airy, useless speculations of philosophy, which,
indeed, obscure those simple truths. That man is endowed
with Reason needs no speculation; since man does not abide
by Reason, he is fit subject for satire. Man's Reason, composed
of his Understanding and Will, is dethroned.

[1] Casaubon, *op. cit.*, pp. 115, 173.

For Understanding rul'd not, and the Will
Heard not her lore, both in subjection now
To sensual appetite, who from beneathe
Usurping over sovran Reason claim'd
Superior sway. . . .[2]

Nor can philosophy, for all its systems, enthrone it again. In his satire on philosophy, therefore, Swift collates man's philosophical systems with his behavior and finds that error is the only relationship between them. Swift's themes in his satire on philosophy in *A Tale of a Tub* are madness and depravity, the madness of man's beclouded Understanding as he concocts systems of philosophy, and the depravity of his vitiated will as he engages in systems of behavior. And madness is no cure for depravity.

I

Madness is the result of vapors.[3]

Whosoever pleases to look into the Fountains of Enthusiasm, from whence, in all Ages, have eternally proceeded such fatning Streams, will find the Spring Head to have been as *troubled* and *muddy* as the Current; Of such great Emolument, is a Tincture of this *Vapour*, which the World calls *Madness*, that without its Help, the World would not only be deprived of those two great Blessings,

---

[2] John Milton, *Paradise Lost* (IX, 1127-31), in *Student's Milton*, ed., Frank Allen Patterson, New York, 1936, p. 311.

[3] Section I of this chapter is primarily an explication of the "Digression on Madness." All references and quotations from the *Tale* in this section of my study refer to this digression, unless otherwise specified.

It is important that in reading this chapter of my study the reader note that no claim is made that Swift was as learned in philosophy as might appear from the spate of erudition which follows. Many of the philosophical currents discussed in this chapter were in the air, property of any educated man; much of the material and many of the attitudes Swift may have derived from secondary sources and have known only in a cursory and fragmentary way. My point is that unless we succeed, systematically and historically, in recreating the philosophical milieu of the time in which Swift wrote the *Tale*, we shall not understand clearly what it is that Swift was satirizing, and the "Digression on Madness" as well as certain other sections of the *Tale* will remain obscure.

Conquests and *Systems,* but even all Mankind would unhappily be reduced to the same Belief in Things Invisible.

And since madness breeds great revolutions and revolutionaries[4] in religion, philosophy, and government, it is proper that brother Jack be of a madness closely correspondent to the madness of the Enthusiastic religion,[5] government, and philosophy. Between Jack and the mad government of King Louis, the mad religion of the Aeolists, and the mad philosophy of Epicurus, there is the close correspondence of a binding *Weltstoff,* Air. This air exists in various modifications; as wind worshiped by the Aeolists; as prime constituent of the tripartite airy soul of Epicureanism; or, indeed, as air deflected, solidified, and turned *fistula in ano* of King Louis. Much in *A Tale of a Tub* is of air, and much is of madness, and all is of a marvelous method.

The state of air in the mad microcosm in the "Digression on Madness" is vaporous. Jack was mad by reason of the vapors; his understanding "was troubled and overspread by Vapours ascending from the lower faculties." It is to be noted, furthermore, that these vapors shook the delicate mechanism of his brain; they resulted in "a Disturbance or transposition of the Brain"; Jack's brain, like Wotton's "hath undergone an unlucky Shake"; his "intellectuals were overturned and his brain shaken out of its natural position." But although Swift's explanation of madness, vapors causing

[4] The concept of the connection between madness and greatness is of respectable antiquity. Plato divided madness into pathological and inspired categories. Aristotle asked, "Why is it that all men who are outstanding in philosophy, poetry or the arts are melancholic . . . ? (Aristotle, *Problems* (xxx, 1), ed., W. S. Hett, London, 1937, II, 155.

The idea is pervasive in Burton's *Anatomy of Melancholy.*

[5] See: Samuel Butler, *Hudibras* (Part II, Canto III, 773-76), in *Poetical Works of Samuel Butler,* ed., Reginald Brimley Johnson, London, 1893, I, 211.

> "As wind i' th' hypochondries pent
> Is but a blast if downward sent,
> But if it upwards chance to fly
> Becomes new light and prophecy;"

mechanical disturbance, is simple, his satirical implications are complex. The clues to Swift's satiric intentions in the "Digression on Madness" lie in the devious intermingling of contemporary philosophical and scientific thought.

That illness was primarily organic in its origins was an idea as old as Aristotle.[6] But it was not until the development of the Iatrophysical (Iatromechanical) school of medicine of the seventeenth century, notably represented by Descartes, that illness was explained in purely mechanical terms.[7] Then illness was considered the expression of a physical impediment to the correct functioning of the body. Especially as applied to mental pathology, Iatrophysical Medicine was logical and simple,[8] a situation extremely comfortable to the satirist of man's madness. The mind, like the rest of the body, was considered a fine and precise machine, easily anatomized for a diagnosis and a cure. While the delicate mechanism of his brain operates properly, man is sweetly reasonable. Shake his upper regions, and their connections, upset his Cartesian pipe-lines,[9] overturn his "intellectuals," and he is mad.

Swift's vapors in "The Digression on Madness," agents of the disturbance called madness (for "every species thereof proceeds from a redundancy of vapors") are of varied origins. Before modern pneumatic chemistry, vapor was as nebulous in definition as in substance. Thus, the soul, for example, although primarily considered air, was also called smoke, wind, breath, exhalation, or vapor. Until the time of the differentiation of the various airs and gases, vapor was described as a kind of, or ingredient of air. In that vapor may

[6] Gregory Zilboorg and George W. Henry, *History of Medical Psychology*, New York, 1941, p. 55.

[7] Albert H. Buck, *Growth of Medicine from the Earliest Times to about 1800*, New Haven, 1917, pp. 366-68, 420.

Fielding H. Garrison, *Introduction to the History of Medicine*, Philadelphia, 1922, pp. 256-59.

[8] Zilboorg and Henry, *op. cit.*, p. 275.

[9] Sir Michael Foster, *Lectures on the History of Physiology*, Cambridge, 1924, p. 266.

be considered, loosely, a kind of air, it may be traced as far back as the original *Weltstoff* of the Hylozoists, subsequently to the essence of the soul as *anima, pneuma,* or *spiritus,* later to the natural, vital, and animal spirits, and even to the archaeus.[10] Swift's vapors in *A Tale of a Tub* and these phenomena are related in that they are all airy and insubstantial in nature. They are more vitally connected in that, in one way or another, they are the answer to the quest for originals, the Original of all Things, the nature of the soul, the connection between God and man, and, indeed, the original of madness. Since Swift's vapors are the original of madness, of man's confusion and perversity in departing from the reasonable order of the world, the connotations of his satire are widely extended. For air, originally bearing largely philosophical connotations, by the sixteenth and seventeenth centuries bore physical and medical connotations too. The new physics of air, just in its cradle (though Wotton thought, "there is scarce any one Body, whose Theory is now so near being compleated as that of the Air")[11] was called the *Science of Pneumaticks.*[12] The new physiology of respiration and the circulation of the blood depended upon air.[13] Vapor, once synonym to breath, soul, spirit, was scarcely a barren point on which to base a satire of man's confusion and perversity. Swift's skill lay in his loading of these vapors, however implicitly, with philosophical and scientific overtones.

Nor did a contemporary reader necessarily need to see any

---

[10] James Mark Baldwin, ed., *Dictionary of Philosophy and Psychology,* New York, 1905-1911, *"anima," "pneuma,"* "spirit," "soul." In ancient Greek philosophy and in Hebrew religion the *pneuma* was used to signify wind, breath, air, soul, and even the mediating principle between God and the world. In medicine the *pneuma* was used in the explanation of the circulation of the blood and functioning of the brain.

For a thorough explanation of medical pneumatism see: Sir T. Clifford Allbutt, *Greek Medicine in Rome,* London, 1921, Chaps. X, XI.

[11] Wotton, *Reflections,* p. 242.

[12] See *O.E.D.* for the development in the meaning of the word *pneumatics.*

[13] Foster, *op. cit.,* pp. 25-53, 172-97.

satirical implications to the vapors. *Qua* vapors, of any definition, they were the orthodox original of madness.[14] That
broad and shifting agglomeration of philosophical and scientific concepts, synthesis of ancient and medieval systems, which
considered man microcosm to the universe, composed of body,
soul, and spirits, created of the four elements each with its
distinctive humor and quality, was only partly less conventional in Swift's day than it was in Shakespeare's. Between
man's body and soul lay the intermediary spirits, airy in substance. The four humours, existing in the blood, and nourished
by food, in their path through the body created those airy
substances, the spirits; successively, the natural spirits (controlling man's vegetative powers and under the domination
of the liver); the vital spirits (controlling man's sensitive
powers and under the domination of the heart); and finally
the animal spirits (controlling man's rational powers and
under the domination of the brain). Thus the orderly progress of the humours in normal functioning. Even in normal
functioning a man might have a preponderance of a certain
humour lending him his distinctive temperament; so that
one might be distinctively choleric, for example, without being
mad. But a humour might be excessive enough to cause madness. Or, instead of reaching the brain after successive steps
and transformations, a humour might rise suddenly to the
brain as vapor, and cause madness. Or a humour might pu-
trefy. Or, indeed, a humour might burn, or grow "adust."
In King Henry IV, prototype of the mad government in *A
Tale of a Tub*, and herald of Sigmund Freud, "the collected
part of the Semen, raised and enflamed, became adust, con-

[14] See the following:

Lily B. Campbell, *Shakespeare's Tragic Heroes, Slaves of Passion*,
Cambridge, 1930, pp. 52 ff.

E. M. W. Tillyard, *Elizabethan World Picture*, London, 1943, pp. 63 ff.

For the persistence of this world picture into the seventeenth century,
see Robert Burton's *Anatomy of Melancholy*.

verted to Choler, turned head upon the spinal Duct, and ascended to the Brain"; whereupon Henry turned Enthusiast in government.

Furthermore, it is significant that Cartesian mechanism could easily be superimposed upon Galenical humours and Hippocratic spirits.[15] One of the few important contemporary works on cerebral pathology, Thomas Willis's *Cerebri Anatome* (1659), in tone reflects the "Digression on Madness," and in spirit derives from the concept of the humours and from Descartes alike.

Wherefore we may far more rightly according to our hypothesis, say that these spirits [animal], emitted from the flame of the blood, are like rays of light, at least these joined with those of wind and air. For just as light is moulded to the impressions of all visible things, and air is moulded to the impression of all audible things, so the animal spirits receive the images impressed on them, not only of the above, but also of odours and all tangible qualities, and deposit them in the common sensorium. But the air or aerial particles, so long as they are free and unmixed, create no rush or tumult, yet when closely confined in clouds, or in machines, or brought into contact with sulphureous and other elastic corpuscles, being forthwith made wild, burst forth into often dreadful meteors, namely winds, whirlwinds and thunder. In the same way the animal spirits, so long as they are pure and are carried in the open spaces of the brain, and its appendages, behave tranquilly enough, but when shut up within muscles, and these permeated with sulphureous particles from the blood, and sometimes with heterogeneous matter in other places, become exceedingly impetuous, that is elastic, or spasmodic.[16]

Swift could have found such highly mechanical explanations

---

[15] Foster, *op. cit.*, pp. 270, 172-97.

See also: René Descartes, *Passions of the Soul*, in *Descartes Selections* ed., Ralph M. Eaton, New York, 1927, p. 365: "We know that all these movements on the muscles, as also all the senses, depend on the nerves, which resemble small filaments, or little tubes, which all proceed from the brain, and thus contain like it a certain very subtle air or wind which is called the animal spirits."

[16] Foster, *op. cit.*, p. 272 (quoting Thomas Willis).

of madness no less Enthusiastic than he found the systems of religion, philosophy, and government that were the products of that madness. For even John Mayow attacked Willis's explanation thus: "Assuredly Fires of this kind and New Lights no less in Anatomy than in Religion appear to me wholly vain and fanatic."[17] And Nicholas Stensen, in a lecture "On the Anatomy of the Brain," criticized Descartes and Willis both, by objecting that they wrote as if "they had mastered with their actual eyes the structure of so admirable a machine and penetrated into the secrets of the great artificer."[18] For here is the very quintessence of Modernism; no longer do speculative thinkers deliberate the inexplicable ways of God to man, an operation metaphysical enough to earn Swift's satire; but they will mechanize the mystery; they will anatomize it; they will prove metaphysics on the anatomical table.[19]

The theory of vapors, however, as it explains the madness of the microcosm, Jack, is only half Swift's concern in his "Digression on Madness." The rest of the digression is devoted to the nature of a mad philosophical system. This system is airy, Epicurean, and, simultaneously, Modern.

Recalling a connection of ancient vintage between madness and greatness, Swift tells us that as the vapors strike the brain, they produce mental prowess. This mental prowess results in revolutions in religion, government, and philosophy. And for speculative philosophy, as for natural philosophy, Swift entertained profound misgivings.

. . . the Philosopher's Way in all Ages has been by erecting certain *Edifices in the Air;* But, whatever Practice and Reputation these kind of Structures have ever formerly possessed, or may still con-

[17] *Ibid.*, p. 277 (quoting John Mayow).

[18] *Ibid.* (quoting Nicholas Stensen).

[19] Swift's most brilliant condemnation of the materialistic explanations of the functioning of the mind, however, is to be found not in the *Tale,* but in the *Mechanical Operation of the Spirit.* See the Guthkelch-Smith edition of the *Tale, Battle,* and *Mechanical Operation,* p. 279.

tinue in, not excepting even that of *Socrates,* when he was suspended in a Basket to help Contemplation; I think, with due Submission, they seem to labour under two Inconveniences. *First,* That the Foundations being laid too high, they have been often out of *Sight,* and ever out of *Hearing. Secondly,* That the Materials, being very transitory, have suffer'd much from Inclemencies of Air. . . .[20]

Furthermore, philosophers are mad because they seek to explain the inexplicable. Then, after convincing themselves of their own systems, they proceed to amass disciples.

For, the Brain, in its natural Position and State of Serenity, disposeth its Owner to pass his Life in the common Forms, without any Thought of subduing Multitudes to his own *Power,* his *Reason* or his *Visions.* . . .

The philosophers' indoctrination of others is, for mechanical reasons, a relatively simple process.

For, there is a peculiar *String* in the Harmony of Human Understanding, which in several individuals is exactly of the same Tuning. This, if you can dexterously screw up to its right Key, and then strike gently upon it; Whenever you have the Good Fortune to light among those of the same Pitch, they will by a secret necessary Sympathy, strike exactly at the same time. And in this one Circumstance, lies all the Skill or luck of the Matter. . . .[21]

[20] *A Tale of a Tub,* p. 56 (Introduction).

[21] This passage in the "Digression on Madness" (p. 167) has many overtones. The word harmony was used medically before it was used philosophically. Furthermore, this passage, which introduces Swift's satire on Epicureanism, already heralds the theme, for the material soul of Epicurus conflicted sharply with the earlier, non-materialistic soul of Aristoxenus, who considered the soul "a condition of 'harmony' of the whole body." (See: Cyril Bailey, *Greek Atomists and Epicurus,* Oxford, 1928, p. 386, n. 3.)

The phenomenon of sympathetic vibration which Swift's passage seems to suggest, though originally discovered by Galileo, was advanced during Swift's lifetime by Mersenne, who also discovered overtones. This phenomenon was reported in the *Philosophical Transactions* of the Royal Society in 1677. (See: A. Wolf, *History of Science, Technology, and Philosophy in the 16th and 17th Centuries,* London, 1935, pp. 281-84.)

The general idea in Swift's passage, expressed in much the same way,

And so, tuned as we are like a lute, if our pitch be correspondent to the philosopher's, we become his disciple. Then discord follows. Then there reigns a harmony of error, an order of disorder, a sympathetic vibration of madness.

But the permutations of possible pitches through which we may achieve harmony with philosophers are not so various that the world lacks "introducers of new schemes of Philosophy," or their disciples. One such philosopher was Apollonius of Tyana,[22] of minor fame, who probably earned his place in Swift's galaxy of mad philosophers by reason of his mysticism, spiritually akin as he was to some Modern occult philosophers. Paracelsus, the Modern, is also a self-evident choice. Swift's selection of Descartes as one of the chief Modern candidates for Bedlam is easily explained too. The point Swift makes in the "Digression on Madness" is that "Cartesius reckoned to see before he died the Sentiments of all Philosophers like so many lesser stars in his Romantick[23] System rapt

may be found in Thomas Willis's *Cerebri Anatome*, 1659 (quoted by Foster, *op. cit.*, pp. 273-74):

" 'So that the ducts of the nervous structures, like cords lightly strung, are extended from the brain and its appendages in every direction to all peripheral parts. And these are so strung and so actuated by a certain continuity of the soul (the corporeal soul), that if either extremity be struck, the blow is forthwith felt throughout the whole. Hence any intention conceived within the brain immediately carries out the purposed work in the proper member or part, and *vice versâ*, any impulse or blow which is inflicted from without on any member or sensitive organ is immediately communicated to the brain. When the impression or impetus passes outwards from the brain along the nerves to motor structures, movement is produced. If on the other hand the impression started from without is carried inwards towards the brain, sensation is the result.' "

See also: Sir Thomas Browne, *Pseudodoxia Epidemica* (Book VII, Chap. 18), in *Works of Sir Thomas Browne*, ed., Charles Sayle, Edinburgh, 1912, III, 79ff.

[22] Temple, *Essay*, p. 451: "That vain sophist Apollonius, (who was but an ape of the ancient philosophers). . . ."

[23] Temple, *Some Thoughts on Reviewing the Essay*, p. 488: Neither the philosophy of Descartes, who "among his friends, always called his philosophy his romance," Amadis, nor the prophecies of Nostradamus were intended for "true stories."

and drawn within his own Vortex." He hoped, Swift implied, by a vortical concourse of men's opinions to win disciples to his method, to be taken for a philosopher rather than for a madman. Or perhaps Swift lamented that so foolish were men, and so madly attuned the pitch of their brains, that by and large, already in the 1690's, Descartes had achieved his aim.

Much more elaborate, however, is Swift's relegation of Epicurus and his disciples Diogenes and Lucretius[24] to the realm of mad philosophers. Their place in the Ancients and Moderns controversy is not at all anomalous once we recognize the simple fact of the neo-Epicurean revival in England in the latter half of the seventeenth century, a revival which turned Epicureanism into a Modern philosophical system.[25] Swift objects that:

Epicurus modestly hoped, that one Time or other, a certain Fortuitous Concourse of all Mens Opinions, after perpetual Justlings, the Sharp with the Smooth, the Light and the Heavy, the Round and the Square, would by certain *Clinamina,* unite in the Notions of *Atoms* and *Void,* as these did in the Originals of all Things.

For the old atomism kindled and enforced the materialism of the New Philosophy; in part it was simultaneously justification and source of Descartes and Hobbes; and it constituted, potentially at least, a real menace to orthodoxy. Epicureanism in the seventeenth century was, in effect, not Ancient at all, having been resuscitated for its atomism and materialism; and whether matter were labeled atomic by the Epicureans or corpuscular by the Cartesians mattered little to the enemy of materialism. Simultaneously with the philosophical revival came the literary revival of Epicureanism in England, and both flourished for half a century and more. But popular

[24] Note that Swift read Lucretius in 1696/7-1697/8. (Thomas Sheridan, *Life of the Rev. Dr. Jonathan Swift,* London, 1787, p. 22.)
[25] Thomas Franklin Mayo, *Epicurus in England,* Texas, 1934.
Louis I. Bredvold, *loc. cit.,* p. 420.

though literary Epicureanism was in 1685,[26] by 1692 it was already on the wane. And though philosophical Epicureanism persisted until well into the eighteenth century, in the 1690's it was partially discredited by the orthodox, Cartesians, and Neo-Platonists as atheistic. But from the middle of the century when Epicureanism was revived in England until the end of the century, there was as much alignment and realignment of forces about Epicureanism as there was about Hobbism and Cartesianism.[27] *A Tale of a Tub*, however, certainly stems from the orthodox opposition to philosophical Epicureanism of the 90's rather than from the enthusiasm for *libertin*, or literary Epicureanism of the 80's. To see Swift as sympathetic to Epicureanism out of respect to Temple, or out of devotion to Antiquity, is to miss the central point of the religious orthodoxy of *A Tale of a Tub* and the satirical system of the "Digression on Madness."

Swift knew his Epicurus well. He knew about the atoms and the void, the clinamin, the types of atoms forming gross as opposed to the finer matter of the soul. But above all he was persuaded that Epicureanism was foolish and a breeder of fools, happy though they might be. It is to be noted that Swift does not attack Epicureanism as materialistic or atheistic. He attacks it as moral philosophy, and uses its pychology to discredit its ethic. He achieves this by pitting Epicureanism against a kind of neo-Stoicism, like Montaigne's

[26] In 1685 appeared Dryden's translation of parts of Lucretius, St. Evremond's *Reflections upon the Doctrine of Epicurus*, and Temple's *Gardens of Epicurus*.

[27] Mayo, *op. cit.*, pp. 56-57, 113, 197, 211. Dr. Mayo considers that Swift was gentle to Epicurus in the *Tale* out of deference to Temple. Except for some well-tempered quotations from Lucretius, chosen generally with a fine eye for their suggestive undertones, and scarcely significant philosophically, it is hard to see where Swift's gentleness lay. Dr. Mayo also seems to suggest that Swift and Temple, in their lack of orthodoxy, approved of Epicurus for his Antiquity. My point is that Swift disliked Epicurus for his Modernity, and that Swift was completely orthodox in the *Tale*, as he claimed to be.

for example, which in its moralistic bias was congenial to him.[28] And he finds Epicurean imperturbability exclusive of Stoical Reason. The most masterly portion of the "Digression on Madness" is the elaborate anatomy of the Epicurean concept of happiness as the greatest good, "the sublime and refined Point of Felicity, called, *the Possession of being well-deceived*; The Serene Peaceful State of being a Fool among Knaves."

That conventional world picture of the sixteenth and seventeenth centuries which portrayed man as composed of body, soul, and spirits, included a psychology which was very consistent with its metaphysic. Man had three souls (or three powers of the one soul): the vegetable soul, common to men, animals, and vegetables, was concerned with growth; the sensitive soul, common to men and animals, was concerned with sensation and simple apprehension; and the chief soul, possessed of man alone and link between him and heaven, was the rational soul, concerned with intellection. Although the descriptions of the operation of the faculties of the mind vary considerably, basically they establish a progression from the senses to the Understanding. Lowest were the external senses which reported the results of sensation, after some rudimentary organization, to the middle faculties, the Memory and the Imagination. The Memory acted as repository of images for future reference. The Imagination, described in very many different ways, was principally considered a recording and repository faculty as well as an inventive faculty of dreams and vision.[29] From the middle faculties proceeded the materials to the Reason, for final disposition. Then intellection was complete. Nevertheless, the Will, counterpart

[28] Quintana, *op. cit.*, pp. 59-62.

[29] According to Plato the imagination supplied dreams and visions; but according to Aristotle the imagination also, like the memory, received, retained, and recalled sensible images. (Clarence deWitt Thorpe, *Aesthetic Theory of Thomas Hobbes*, Ann Arbor, Michigan, 1940, p. 129.)

to the Understanding in the composite faculty called the Reason, was free to follow the recommendations of the Understanding or not, as it proceeded to initiate action.[30]

But the whole operation of man's rational soul was so elaborate and delicate that, as in a machine with many moving parts, the possible sources for error were manifold. Any one of the faculties might err. The orderly progress of intellection might be disturbed, to be followed by discord "when a man's fancy gets *astride* on his Reason, when Imagination is at Cuffs with the Senses, and common Understanding, as well as common Sense, is kickt out of Doors."

But the whole rational system is constantly imperilled by another complex system, the appetitive powers of the soul, the emotions, or as they were called variously, the *motions* when mild, the *affections* when strong, and the *perturbations* or *passions* when violent. These passions, as Swift called them, were bred in the sensitive soul and thus had intimate connections with the Imagination; but they could confuse all the other faculties of the mind too. They could confuse the senses and turn them into hedonists, so that they acted for their immediate pleasure rather than for the ultimate good. The chief source for error, however, lay in the effects of the passions on the Imagination, and in the Imagination itself lay the greatest potential danger. As a faculty of the sensitive soul under the domination of the heart, the Imagination could most easily be swayed by the passions, and in turn, the Imagination could sway the Will and entice it away from the Understanding.

The knowledge which respecteth the Faculties of the Mind of man is of two kinds; the one respecting his Understanding and Reason, and the other his Will, Appetite, and Affection; whereof the former produceth Position or Decree, the latter Action or Execution. It is true that the Imagination is an agent or *nuncius* in both prov-

[30] For the materials in this and the following paragraphs, see: Lily B. Campbell, *op. cit.*, pp. 65-101.

inces, both the judicial and ministerial. For sense sendeth over
to Imagination before Reason have judged: and Reason sendeth
over to Imagination before the Decree can be acted; for Imagination ever precedeth Voluntary Motion: saving that this Janus
of Imagination hath differing faces; for the face towards Reason
hath the print of Truth, but the face towards Action hath the print
of Good; which nevertheless are faces

Quales decet esse sororum,

(sister faces). Neither is the Imagination simply and only a mes-
senger; but is invested with or at leastwise usurpeth no small
authority in itself, besides the duty of the message. For it was well
said by Aristotle, *That the mind hath over the body that commandment, which the lord hath over a bondman; but that reason hath
over the imagination that commandment which a magistrate hath
over a free citizen;* who may come also to rule in his turn.[31]

Thus the Reason was in constant danger of rebellion from the
lower faculties since it had to work directly through them,
and they were easily affected by the passions. It could, indeed,
happen that the passions swayed the Reason directly, and then
even greater discord followed.

This psychological picture, however, was viewed from two
distinct *foci,* depending upon whether the Peripatetic or the
Stoic bias was the stronger. The Stoics saw only danger, enmity
to the Reason, in the passions. The Peripatetics, however,
found the passions bad only when excessive or uncontrolled;
and their approach was being justified by the new psychology
of the seventeenth century, and especially by Hobbes. For
Hobbes the passions were scarcely evil, nor did they conflict
with the Understanding, any more than the Imagination conflicted with the Understanding. The passions and the Imagination were productive and led to advancement in knowledge.[32]

Desire, to know why, and how, [is] CURIOSITY; such as is in no

---

[31] Sir Francis Bacon, *Advancement of Learning,* in *Philosophical Works
of Francis Bacon,* ed., John M. Robertson, New York, 1905, p. 110.

(All other works of Sir Francis Bacon cited in this study will refer to
this edition.)

[32] Thorpe, *op. cit., passim.*

living Creature but *Man;* so that Man is distinguished, not only by his Reason; but also by this singular Passion from other *Animals;.* . . which is a Lust of the Mind, that by a preseverance of delight in the continuall and indefatigable generation of Knowledge, exceedeth the short vehemence of any carnall pleasure.

. . . a slow Imagination, maketh that Defect, or fault of the mind, which is commonly called DULNESSE, *Stupidity,* and sometimes by other names that signifie slowness of motion, or difficulty to be moved.[33]

In satire of this unconventional attitude, Swift wrote:

Now, he that will examine Human Nature with Circumspection enough, may discover several *Handles,* whereof the *Six* Senses afford one apiece, beside a great Number that are screw'd to the Passions, and some few riveted to the Intellect. Among these last, *Curiosity* is one, *Curiosity,* that Spur in the side, that Bridle in the Mouth, that Ring in the Nose, of a lazy, and impatient, and a grunting Reader. By this *Handle* it is, that an Author should seize upon his Readers; which as soon as he hath once compast, all Resistance and struggling are in vain; and they become his Prisoners as close as he pleases, till Weariness or Dulness force him to let go his Gripe.[34]

Thus Swift satirizes Hobbes, his championship of the passions and the Imagination, reputable agents of Curiosity and Quickness; and in the "sixth sense" Swift recalls Hobbes's internal sense for discriminating the passions of the mind.[35]

But wherever the emphasis lay, whether the passions were feared or tolerated, and precarious though the whole conventional psychological system was, it served, nevertheless, as explanation of man's evil and provided a moralistic system through which man could be urged towards virtue, by following that supreme and divine faculty, Reason. In contrast to this system, the Epicurean psychological system was simple and suspicious to a Christian moralist oppressed by man's per-

[33] Thomas Hobbes, *Leviathan* (I, 6, 8), ed., A. D. Lindsay, New York, 1937, pp. 26, 33.
[34] *A Tale of a Tub,* p. 203 (Section XI).
[35] Thorpe, *op. cit.,* p. 136.

versity and filled with a lively appreciation of the difficulty of bringing him to virtue. Nor was Swift convinced of the identification between Christian virtue and Epicurean happiness made by Temple and other admirers of Epicurus.

The Epicurean soul is mortal and material, a body made up of fine atoms of air of three types and a fourth element of super-fine atoms, the soul of the soul, which upon a man's death dissolve into smoke. Epicureanism neither affirms nor denies the earlier division of the soul into rational and irrational categories. But this is certain, in Epicureanism the hegemony of the Reason, chief function of the rational soul, is overthrown and Sensation put in its place. It is difficult to overemphasize the importance of Sensation in Epicureanism, any more than in Hobbism. Sensation is basic, sole intermediary between man and the universe, sole criterion and guarantee of truth, incapable of error, and antecedent to all the functions of the mind. Sensation can neither be checked nor superseded. The mind, in all its operations, imitates, and depends upon Sensation whose images it interprets and classifies. Reason is a process of addition by which stored images, resulting from Sensation, are combined. Insofar as addition and comparison are fallible, Reason is fallible; but Sensation is always true.[36] Like Swift, Meric Casaubon saw the Modern philosopher as "a brutish *Epicure* who would not have us to believe either Sun or Moon to be bigger then they appear to our eyes, lest we should in any thing adscribe more to reason, then to sense: and yet elsewhere denieth that the eye was made to see, or the ear to hear. . . lest he might seem to adscribe somewhat to providence."[37]

The Memory, conventionally "more wonderfull by far [than the Imagination], though commonly lesse wondered

[36] Bailey, *op. cit.*, Part II, Chap. 2 ("Canonice"), Chap. 8 ("The Soul, Sensation, Thought, and Will").
Lucretius, *De Rerum Natura*, ed., W. H. D. Rouse, London, 1928.
[37] Casaubon, *op. cit.*, p. 73.

at, (as the fashion is amongst the vulgar of men),"[38] according to Epicureanism, operates by stacking the images derived from Sensation, which it keeps in "anticipation." In the erroneous stacking of these images lies the margin for error of the Memory. The Imagination, a faculty which is not analyzed very carefully in the Epicurean system, emerges as a far more reputable faculty of the mind than the seventeenth century, up to Hobbes's time, was willing to concede it; it is a super-subtle kind of Sensation in which *eidola* impinge directly upon it rather than upon the senses. Indeed, Swift's condemnation of the Imagination, like his condemnation of the Passions, is directed against Hobbism rather than Epicureanism. In a period when the Imagination was closely related to Enthusiasm,[39] Hobbes treated the Imagination as a natural and useful faculty, a source of poetry and truth, and a faculty that could be trusted to operate harmoniously with the Reason and the Passions.[40] Under the influence of Hobbes, Dryden had cautioned: "No man should pretend to write, who cannot temper his fancy with his judgment: nothing is more dangerous to a raw horseman, than a hot-mouthed jade without a curb."[41] To which Swift replied, apologetically, at the end of the "Digression on Madness": "I . . . am a Person, whose Imaginations are hard-mouth'd and exceedingly disposed to run away with his *Reason*, which I have observed from long Experience, to be a very light Rider, and easily shook off." The jade Imagination is the same, but his Reason, Swift implies, is not as trustworthy as Dryden's and Hobbes's judgment.

[38] *Ibid.*, p. 46.
[39] George Williamson, "Restoration Revolt against Enthusiasm," *Studies in Philology*, XXX, 571-603 (Oct., 1933).
[40] Thorpe, *op. cit.*, p. 23.
[41] John Dryden, "Preface to Troilus and Cressida, Containing the Grounds of Criticism in Tragedy (1679)," *Essays of John Dryden*, ed., W. P. Kerr, Oxford, 1926, I, 222.

827
S977yn
69-1396

As Swift sees Epicureanism, however, in the "Digression on Madness" (even though he strays out of the framework to attack Hobbism on a few occasions), it is dangerously perverse. Swift's happy Epicurean has dethroned Reason, exalted the Imagination, deprecated the Memory, and given the Senses supremacy. He has upset the conventional hierarchy. He has divorced truth to espouse fiction.

... 'tis manifest, what mighty Advantages Fiction has over Truth; and the Reason is just at our Elbow; because Imagination can build nobler Scenes, and produce more wonderful Revolutions than Fortune or Nature will be at Expence to furnish. Nor is Mankind so much to blame in his Choice, thus determining him, if we consider that the Debate meerly lies between *Things past,* and *Things conceived;* and so the Question is only this; Whether Things that have Place in the *Imagination,* may not as properly be said to *Exist,* as those that are seated in the *Memory;* which may be justly held in the Affirmative, and very much to the Advantage of the former, since This is acknowledged to be the *Womb* of Things, and the other allowed to be no more than the *Grave.*

Just as the Imagination presents prettier fictions than the Memory to the Epicurean, so he prefers the Senses which dwell on the "Superficies of things" to the Reason.

In the Proportion that Credulity is a more peaceful Possession of the Mind, than Curiosity, so far preferable is that Wisdom, which converses about the Surface, to that pretended Philosophy which enters into the Depth of Things, and then comes back gravely with Informations and Discoveries, that in the inside they are good for nothing. The two Senses, to which all Objects first address themselves, are the Sight and the Touch; These never examine farther than the Colour, the Shape, the Size, and whatever other Qualities dwell, or are drawn by Art upon the Outward of Bodies; and then comes Reason officiously, with Tools for cutting, and opening, and mangling, and piercing, offering to demonstrate, that they are not of the same consistence quite thro! Now, I take all this to be the last Degree of perverting Nature; one of whose Eternal Laws it is, to put her best Furniture forward. And therefore, in order to save the Charges of all such expensive Anatomy

[41]

Alverno College Library
Milwaukee, Wisconsin

for the Time to come; I do here think fit to inform the Reader, that in such Conclusions as these, Reason is certainly in the Right; and that in most Corporeal Beings, which have fallen under my Cognizance, the *Outside* hath been infinitely preferable to the *In*: Whereof I have been farther convinced from some late Experiments. Last Week I saw a Woman *flay'd*, and you will hardly believe, how much it altered her Person for the worse.[42]

Therefore:

He that can with *Epicurus* content his Ideas with the *Films* and *Images* that fly off upon his Senses from the *Superficies* of Things; Such a Man truly wise, creams off Nature, leaving the Sower and the Dregs, for Philosophy and Reason to lap up. This is the sublime and refined Point of Felicity called, *the Possession of being well deceived*; The Serene Peaceful State of being a Fool among Knaves.[43]

This it is to prefer credulity, leading to fiction, and product of the Imagination and the Senses, to curiosity, leading to truth, and product of the Reason. This it is to be happy; to live in a fool's paradise; to have the ethic and psychology of an Epicurean; to be serenely and imperturbably well-deceived. Swift's satire is directed against the ethical end of Epicureanism, happiness, serenity, imperturbability. Indeed Epicurus was more a moralist than a metaphysician. The atoms falling fortuitously in the void absolved man of every shred of determinism, responsibility, and even his own destiny. And the ethical end of Epicureanism, justified by its physics, is extremely consistent with its psychology. As Swift saw neo-Epicureanism, it insisted upon an atomic and materialistic soul, long comfortably incorporeal. It discredited a Reason long undisputed monarch and buttressed by a growing rationalism, by a Sensation long since associated with error and the "shadows of the Cave," now, somehow, perversely become omnipotent, omniscient, and infallible. Contemporary science, in-

[42] Note that "Reason is certainly in the Right," is obviously an error; the whole context proves that Swift meant that Reason is in the *wrong*.
[43] *Philosophy* here is undoubtedly *moral* philosophy.

deed, endorsed Swift's mistrust of the senses, at the same time
that contemporary philosophy exalted them. The new optics,
for example, with its discoveries of new theories of light
and color, of refraction, inverted images, the theory of the
accommodation of lenses,[44] suggested that not only were things
not what they seemed, but very likely often what they seemed
not to be. The Memory, "mother of the Muses," long respectable as a repository of things as they happened, and surely
more trustworthy than the Imagination, at least partially
repository of things as they might be, is discredited too, and
the past becomes questionable as remembered, and the imaginary a pure and direct vision.

Because, *Memory* being an Employment of the Mind upon things
past, is a Faculty for which the Learned in our Illustrious Age,
have no manner of Occasion, who deal entirely with *Invention*,
and strike all Things out of themselves, or at least, by Collision,
from each other. . . .[45]

The growing mistrust of the Imagination, constantly suspected
of relations with the Passions, and increasingly suspected of
Enthusiasm,[46] finds no support in the Epicurean psychology.

Neo-Stoicism, on the other hand, in its insistence upon the
supreme power of the Reason to guide man towards virtue,
involved a constant warfare in man's soul between his Reason
and his lower faculties, between his Reason and his Passions.
According to its tenets man could scarcely remain imperturb-
able, and happiness was not his business on earth. His business
was constantly to fight Reason's battles and keep its fortress
impregnable. To one devoted to this ethic, Epicureanism

[44] See the following:
  Wolf, *op. cit.*, pp. 244-74.
  Elsie C. Graham, *Optics and Vision*, New York, 1929, Chaps. 2, 3:
Miss Graham points out the importance of the Epicurean theory of vision
in promoting seventeenth century innovations in optics; the Epicurean
theory helped, ironically enough, to promote a theory which ran counter
to it.
[45] *A Tale of a Tub*, p. 135 (Section VI).
[46] Williamson, *loc. cit., passim.*

was a betrayal. For to what did its psychology amount? To an Epicurean ethic, the ethic of happiness, the ethic of the fool, of the mad, Modern philosopher of the "Digression on Madness." Much of the "savage indignation" in *A Tale of a Tub* is the exasperation of the militant moralist at the serene imperturbability of the happy sinner.

II

In surveying Antiquity the defender of Ancient learning cut away all its lunatic fringes and retained what was most sane and durable. But in criticizing Modernity, he took into account all the currents swirling about him, muddy or clear; and in satirizing Modernity he paid particular attention to what was muddiest. Modern occultism was of a pervasive muddiness, a muddiness which Swift exploited in the clearest detail in his satire on Modern occultism in *A Tale of a Tub*, the Aeolist system, based principally upon the *Anthroposophia Theomagica* of Thomas Vaughan, alias Eugenius Philalethes.

If we extend by a little the words of Eugenius Philalethes —"a witch is a rebel in physics and a rebel is a witch in politics"[47]—so that by a witch we mean an occultist, and by a political nonconformist we also mean a religious one, we shall see the satirical method of Section VIII of *A Tale of a Tub*, a disquisition on the doctrine and discipline of Aeolism. For through Aeolism Swift discredits religious and political Enthusiasm by philosophical Enthusiasm, occultism. Although Swift's primary purpose in his Aeolist system is to satirize Nonconformity, the method of his satire is incorporated in a philosophical system, even as his satire on Modern philosophy and his satire on man's behavior are incorporated in philosophical systems. Thus the mad nonconformist state of the Aeolists is windy, Modern, and occult. Jack, the mad-

---

[47] Thomas Vaughan, *Anthroposophia Theomagica*, in *Works of Thomas Vaughan: Eugenius Philalethes*, ed., Arthur Edward Waite, London, 1919, p. 35. (All works of Thomas Vaughan hereafter cited in this study will be understood to come from this edition, unless otherwise noted.)

man by reason of the vapors, established Aeolism on the ruling principle of wind, air in its most destructive state, air in motion. And among the Aeolists wind was all in all—God, universe, man, soul, spirit, body.

The learned *Aeolists* maintain the Original Cause of all Things to be *Wind*, from which Principle this whole Universe was first produced, and into which it must at last be resolved; that the same Breath which had kindled, and blew *up* the Flame of Nature, should one day blow it *out*. . . . This is what the *Adepti* understand by their *Anima Mundi*; that is to say, the *Spirit*, or *Breath*, or *Wind* of the World.[48]

Philosophical occultism, and indeed, practical occultism too, when related to their primary intentions, had a consuming interest in deciphering the mystery of the Universe. Whether philosophically cabalistical and preoccupied with the Creation; or philosophically hermetical and devoted to tracing the magical correspondences between the macrocosm and the microcosm; whether practically theurgic and obsessed with wonder-working; or practically alchemical and obsessed with finding an evolutionary process—all occultism may be traced to an ultimate quest for the original of all things; a quest of which the ultimate aim was the achievement of universal systems.[49] Accomplished in all the major aspects of the occultism of his day was Thomas Vaughan, *illuminatus, vere adep-*

[48] *A Tale of a Tub*, pp. 150, 151 (Section VIII).

(All quotations from and references to the *Tale* in Section II of this Chapter will refer, unless otherwise noted, to Section VIII of the *Tale*, pp. 150-61.)

[49] See the following:

Arthur Edward Waite, ed., *Works of Thomas Vaughan*, London, 1919, Introduction.

Arthur Edward Waite, ed., *Magical Writings of Thomas Vaughan*, London, 1888, Introductory Essay.

Arthur Edward Waite, *Occult Sciences*, New York, 1923.

Arthur Edward Waite, *Holy Kabbalah*, New York, 1929.

John Read, *Prelude to Chemistry*, London, 1936.

Arthur John Hopkins, *Alchemy, Child of Greek Philosophy*, New York, 1934.

Rebecca Price, *Studies in Thomas Vaughan*, 1942. (An unpublished Columbia University Master's Essay.)

tus, and perhaps even *magus.*[50] And like many of his contemporaries, Swift knew well at least Vaughan's *Anthroposophia Theomagica.* As cosmic philosopher and practical alchemist, Vaughan was interested in the *anima mundi* on both scores.

The normal, celestial, ethereal part of man is that whereby we do move, see, feel, taste and smell, and have a commerce with all material objects whatsoever. It is the same in us as in beasts, and it is derived from heaven—where it is predominant—to all inferior earthly creatures. In plain terms it is part of the Soul of the World, commonly called the Medial soul because the influences of the Divine Nature are conveyed through it to the more material parts of the creature, with which of themselves they have no proportion. By means of this Medial Soul, or the ethereal nature, man is made subject to the influence of stars and is partly disposed of by the celestial harmony. For this middle spirit—middle, I mean, between both extremes and not that which is in the outward heaven as that which is in man—is of a fruitful, insinuating nature and carried with a strong desire to multiply itself, so that the celestial form stirs up and excites the elemental. For this spirit is in man, in beasts, in vegetables, in minerals; and in everything it is the mediate cause of composition and multiplication.[51]

Thus the *anima mundi* as it operates in the macrocosm and the microcosm. The concept of the correspondence and correlation between man and the universe,[52] as old as speculative philosophy, still flourished in the seventeenth century, though when the concept was merely metaphor is not always easily determined. But for the occultists, the parallels between macrocosm and microcosm were infinitely more than of speculative or metaphorical use; the concept was a magical doctrine; through the examination of the "elementary world," one could decipher the mysteries of the "intelligible world"; man would elucidate God, the body the spirit, and earth

[50] Price, *op. cit., passim.*
[51] Vaughan, *Anthroposophia Theomagica,* pp. 40, 41.
[52] For an excellent treatment of the correspondences, see: Tillyard, *op. cit.,* pp. 78ff.

heaven.[53] So great were the correspondences, as Samuel Butler rejoiced satirically, that "there is not so much as an individual Beard upon the Face of the Earth, that has not another there [in the "intelligible World"] perfectly of the same Colour and Cut to match it."[54] And, therefore, having examined the macrocosm rapidly, Swift turns the focus of his attention to the microcosm.

Just as the universe has its *anima mundi*, its breath, spirit, and wind, so has man.

For whether you please to call the *forma informans* of Man, by the name of *Spiritus, Animus, Afflatus,* or *Anima*; What are all these but several Appelations for *Wind*?

Or, as Vaughan points out, the *anima mundi* is the "Universal Spirit of Nature."[55] As for man's soul, it is:

. . . an essence not to be found in the texture of the great world and therefore merely divine and supernatural. Montanus calls it "Wind of the Divine Spirit and Breath of Divine Life." He seems also to make the Creation of man a little incarnation, as if God in his work had multiplied Himself.[56]

And man, being most windy, Swift decided, is most perfect.

. . . and therefore, *Man* is in highest Perfection of all created Things, as having by the great Bounty of Philosophers, been en-

[53] Waite, *Occult Sciences*, p. 185.
Note, however, that the occultists strained what was a perfectly orthodox and acceptable concept. "The Ancient opinion that man was Microcosmus, an abstract or model of the world, hath been fantastically strained by Paracelsus and the alchemists, as if there were to be found in man's body certain correspondences and parallels, which should have respect to all varieties of things, as stars, planets, minerals, which are extant in the great world. But this much is evidently true, that of all substances which nature hath produced, man's body is the most extremely compounded." (Bacon, *Advancement of Learning*, p. 103.) See also: Bacon, *De Sapientia Veterum*, p. 849.
[54] Samuel Butler, "Hermetic Philosopher," *Genuine Remains of Samuel Butler*, ed., R. Thayer, London, 1759, II, 235.
See also: Butler, *Hudibras* (Part II, Canto III, 225-34), I, 192.
[55] Vaughan, *Anima Magica Abscondita*, p. 78.
[56] Vaughan, *Anthroposophia Theomagica*, p. 33.

dued with three distinct *Anima's* or *Winds*, to which the sage *Aeolists*, with much Liberality, have added a fourth of equal Necessity, as well as Ornament with the other three; by this *quartum Principium* taking in the four Corners of the World; which gave Occasion to that Renowned *Cabbalist*, *Bumbastus*, of placing the Body of Man, in due Position to the four *Cardinal* Points.

That man had three souls, the vegetable, sensible, and rational, Swift did not need the occultists to tell him. (Nor did he ever fail to seize the occasion for a thrust at scholasticism.) But for the fourth soul, the super-spiritual one, he had to look to the occultists, and he found it in the *Anthroposophia Theomagica*.

Lastly, above the rational spirit is the *Mens* or Hidden intelligence, commonly called the illuminated intellect, and of Moses the breath of lives. This is that spirit which God himself breathed into man and by which man is united again to God. . . the Divine Light, flowing into the *Mens* did assimilate and convert the inferior portions of the soul to God. . . .[57]

When Bumbastus divided the body of man into four points, correspondent to the cardinal or geographical points, he was "advancing the microcosmical conceit."[58] But how Swift's occult soul has suddenly turned *"quartum principium"* and basis for the microcosmical geography of Paracelsus is a mystery which even occultism does not unveil.

Nor has man only four souls according to the Aeolists.

Man brings with him into the World a peculiar portion or Grain of *Wind*, which may be called a *Quinta essentia*, extracted from

[57] *Ibid.*, p. 42.

[58] Sir Thomas Browne, *Pseudodoxia Epidemica* (Book II, Chap. III), I, 239-40: "This Opinion confirmed would much advance the Microcosmical Conceit, and commend the Geography of *Paracelsus*, who according to the Cardinal Points of the World divideth the body of man; and therefore working upon humane ordure, and by long preparation rendring it odoriferous, he terms it *Zibeta Occidentalis*, Western *Civet*, making the face the East, but the posteriours the *America* or Western part of his Microcosm." (I am indebted to Guthkelch-Smith, *op. cit.*, p. 351 for this reference.)

For Swift's reference to the *Zibeta Occidentalis*, see *A Tale of a Tub*, p. 165 (Digression on Madness).

the other four. This *Quintessence* is of a Catholick Use upon all Emergencies of Life, . . .

Aristotle's quintessence, drawn from the four elements, was strictly material in character, a materialism the occultists found repugnant; "There is no fifth principle—no quintessence as Aristotle dreamed—but God Almighty," Vaughan insisted.[59] When they did use the term, they preferred to give it highly spiritualized connotations: they called the quintessence, variously, the *"Sphaera Solis,"* "the Heaven and Celestial substance," the " 'ray of the firmament which was flashed through the soul of the World by the voice of the Creator,' " the "Eternal Nature," the "Third Principle and Paradisical Heaven."[60]

Indeed much of Swift's satire on occultism derives from his methodical muddle of spirit and matter, even as the occultists subverted the conventional dichotomy between spirit and matter. "Learn to refer," Vaughan urged, "all naturals to their spirituals by the way of secret analogy; for this is the way the magicians went and found out miracles."[61] Therefore wind was not only soul and spirit to the Aeolists, but it was matter too, *primordium*, or *prima materia*;[62] a first matter the occultists found merely corrupted spirit.[63]

[59] Vaughan, *Anthroposophia Theomagica*, p. 25.

[60] See Appendix F, Guthkelch-Smith, *op. cit.*, p. 351. This note was supplied to the editors by Arthur Edward Waite, who derived it from Rulandus, Paracelsus, and Boehme.

[61] Vaughan, *Anima Magica Abscondita*, p. 116.

[62] Primordial matter was that "from which all things came and to which they reverted," according to practical alchemy, since, if all bodies were composed of varying proportions of the four elements, the bodies could be changed into one another by varying the proportions of the elements. (Read, *op. cit.*, p. 10.)

[63] Waite, ed., *Works of Thomas Vaughan*, pp. xxxii-xxxiii (Introduction). Waite, ed., *Magical Writings of Thomas Vaughan*, p. xvii (Introductory Essay): "They [Vaughan's writings] claim to provide the intelligent reader with a substantially fresh revelation of that mysterious First Matter of the *Opus Magnum* which endows those who know it, and can avail themselves of its manifold potencies, with a full and perfect power for the successful conduct of all classes of theurgic experiment."

That since *Wind* has the Master-Share as well as Operation in every Compound, by Consequence, those Beings must be of chief Excellence, wherein that *Primordium* appears most prominently to abound. . . .

Although the *prima materia,* the "chaos," figures in Vaughan's *Anthroposophia Theomagica* and *Magica Abscondita,* he expounds it (though it is indescribable) more fully later when he had already beheld it (though it is invisible) and tasted it. The *prima materia* had philosophical and practical applications for Vaughan. It was the chief ingredient of the philosopher's stone and the magic elixir; it was not unrelated to "the immediate Catholic character of God Himself in His unity and trinity"; he called it water but he said it was not water; it looked like stone but it was not stone; it was the source of the four elements and the three philosophical principles.[64]

Thus wind, as soul, spirit, body, was an excellent working symbol for Swift in his satire on occultism, an occultism which differentiated its terms so carefully and came to wind. And if Swift found conventional speculative philosophy vain and obscurantist to the point of madness, how much more persuasively could he find the occult philosophy of a pervasive madness! By choosing occultism as the jade on which to ride Nonconformity, he was merely continuing his satire of a "laundress firm in . . . Epicurus," with a "keeper deep in the Rosycrucian principles."[65] As opposed to the void of Epi-

---

[64] Waite, ed., *Works of Thomas Vaughan,* pp. xxxvi-xlii. (The tracts referred to are: *Coelum Terrae, Lumen de Lumine, Euphrates, Magica Adamica, Aula Lucis.* The quotation in the text is from *Coelum Terrae,* p. 193.)

[65] See Chapter 1, *supra.*

See also: Temple, *Some Thoughts on Reviewing the Essay,* p. 506: "For my own part, I confess I have always looked upon alchemy in natural philosophy, to be like enthusiasm in divinity, and to have troubled the world much to the same purpose. And I should as soon fall into the study of Rosycrucian philosophy, and expect to meet a Nymph or a Sylph for a wife or a mistress, as with the elixir for my health, or philosopher's stone for my fortune."

curus, among the Aeolists there is a plenum of wind, in their universe, their gods, and their devils. And the Aeolists are derived from the wind of Antiquity.

In tracing Aeolism to Antiquity, Swift no more impugned the Ancients than he impugned them in deriving Modern critics from Zoilus. He was tracing Modernity to the most questionable aspects of Antiquity and assuring the Moderns, that, as they insisted, they had indeed advanced beyond the Ancients—in madness. Hence he derives Aeolism from the Ancient oracles and "horrid" rites and mysteries of Antiquity, in such great disrepute in the seventeenth century as fountain-heads of Enthusiasm;[66] a derivation, incidentally, rather more historically correct than his derivation of Bentley from Zoilus. Through this derivation of occultism, Swift was able simultaneously to incorporate some broad satire on the reputed promiscuity of the Nonconformists, especially of the "Holy Sisters."[67]

Nor did Swift parody Vaughan's *Anthroposophia Theomagica* exclusively in his system of Aeolism, any more than Samuel Butler parodied Vaughan exclusively in his Character of "An Hermetic Philosopher," though both used Vaughan as prototype of the occult philosopher. Both satirized the whole complex of seventeenth century occultism; an agglomeration of cabalistical and hermetical doctrines, and therefore of mysticism, philosophy, science, pseudo-science, and magic; an agglomeration whose symbols were derived from astronomy, physiology, mythology, folk lore, and indeed any aspect of life in many parts of the world and accumulated over the space of a thousand years and more.[68] In this vague

[66] See: Casaubon, *op. cit.*, Chap. I.

[67] C. M. Webster, "The Puritans' Ears in *A Tale of a Tub*," *Modern Language Notes*, XLVII, 96-97 (Feb., 1932).

C. M. Webster, "Swift's *Tale of a Tub* Compared with Earlier Satires of the Puritans," *Publications of the Modern Language Association*, XLVII, 171-78 (March, 1932).

[68] Price, *op. cit.*, p. 205.

and shifting realm Eugenius Philalethes was preeminent, philosopher, mystic, practical alchemist, Rosicrucian, and perhaps even Satanist that he was. It is true that there were pure freshets in the muddy waters of occultism, since it borrowed much from the clear stream of learning; and Vaughan was among the more serious and learned of his brother *illuminati*. But it is even truer, to the unilluminated eye, that even in Vaughan the nonsense is in the ascendant and easily obfuscates and discredits the sensible. Certainly it must have appeared so to Swift, enemy to Nonconformity and occultism alike, though not in the same measure. And it is well to remember that to one opposed to Nonconformity, the most serious, Protestant, humanistic Nonconformist was discredited not so much by his own theology and politic as by any lunatic sectarian.

And Swift knew enough of the muddy streams of occultism in its practical as well as philosophical manifestations to prove himself, satirically, a *vere adeptus* knowing the *arcanum*, and to incorporate it in *A Tale of a Tub* more than has been suspected. That much of his *arcanum* stems directly either from Vaughan's *Anthroposophia Theomagica*, "a plenary but short inquisition into the mysteries of Nature,"[69] or from Samuel Butler's Character of "An Hermetic Philosopher" does not diminish Swift's illumination.

Out of his "great Affection for the *Modern learned*," Swift presents a recipe, derived from the papers of a "great Philosopher of O. *Brazile*," not merely for an universal elixir, but for "an universal System, in a small portable Volume, of all Things that are to be Known, or Believed, or Imagined, or Practised in Life." If three drops of this highly alchemical elixir be sniffed up the nose:

It will dilate it self about the brain (where there is any) in fourteen Minutes, and you immediately perceive in your Head an infinite

[69] Vaughan, *Anthroposophia Theomagica*, p. 31.

Number of Abstracts, Summaries, Compendiums, Extracts, Collections, Medullas, Excerpta quaedam's, Florilegias, *and the like, all disposed into great Order, and reducible upon Paper.*[70]

That the great "Philosopher of O. Brazile" was a Rosicrucian we can only guess, but we know that the Rosicrucians were *adepti* at alchemical formulae and universal knowledge, and that they kept their recipes purposely obscure. According to Butler, they proceeded to the *arcanum* not via the nose but the stomach.

This Knowledge they affirm, may be attained by Eating, in a planetary Moment, a Rasher made of the Liver of a Cameleon, the only broiled Lexicon in the World. For they will undertake to teach any Kind of mysterious Learning in the World by way of Diet; and therefore have admirable Receipts, to make several Dishes for *Talisman, Magic,* and *Cabal,* in which Sciences a Man of an ingenious Stomach may eat himself into more Knowledge at a meal than he could possibly arrive at by Seven Years Study.[71]

For the "sublime Spirits who shall be appointed to labor in a universal Comment" on *A Tale of a Tub,* Swift drops a few occult "innuendos."

And First, I have couched a very profound Mystery in the Number of O's multiply'd by *Seven,* and divided by *Nine.* Also, if a devout brother of the *Rosy Cross* will pray fervently for sixty-three Mornings, with a lively Faith, and then transpose certain Letters and Syllables according to Prescription, in the second and fifth Section; they will certainly reveal into a full Receit of the *Opus Magnum.* Lastly, Whoever will be at the Pains to calculate the whole Number of each Letter in this Treatise, and sum up the Difference exactly between the several Numbers, assigning the true natural Cause for every such Difference; the Discoveries in the Product, will plentifully reward his Labour. But then he must beware of *Bythus* and *Sigè,* and be sure not to forget the Qualities of *Acamoth: A cujus lacrymis humecta prodit Substantia, à risu lucida, a tristitiâ solida, etc. a timore mobilis*; wherein *Eugenius Philalethes* hath committed an unpardonable Mistake.[72]

[70] *A Tale of a Tub,* pp. 126-27 (Digression in the Modern Kind).
[71] Butler, "Hermetic Philosopher," II, 234.
[72] *A Tale of a Tub,* pp. 186-87 (Section x).

That in his caveat Swift here holds Eugenius accountable for Irenaeus, again does not detract from Swift's illumination.[73]

That "WHITTINGTON *and his Cat* . . . the work of that Mysterious *Rabbi, Jehuda Hannasi,* containing a Defence of the *Gemara* of the *Jerusalem Misna,* and its just preference to that of *Babylon,* contrary to the vulgar Opinion,"[74] shows a certain confusion on Swift's part between the mysticism of the *Mishna* and *Talmud* and the later mysticism of Cabala[75] is a mere detail. All mystical Hebraic writings were easily discredited by Cabala, whose exponents:

. . . have found out, who is the true Owner of the *Beast* in the *Apocalyps,* which has long passed for a Stray among the Learned; what is the true Product of 666, that has rung like *Whittington's* Bells in the Ears of Expositors; how long it is to the day of Judgment, and, which is more wonderful, whether it shall be in Winter or Summer.[76]

For not to be a cabalist (and the term was used so broadly in the seventeenth century as sometimes to be synonymous with occultist) was to be nothing, even if one were Homer.

. . . his Account of the *Opus magnum* is extreamly poor and deficient; he seems to have read but very superficially, either *Sendivog[i]us, Behmen,* or *Anthroposophia Theomagica.* He is also quite mistaken about the *Sphaera Pyroplastica,* a neglect not to be attoned for; and (if the Reader will admit so severe a Censure) *Vix crederem Autorem hunc, unquam audivisse ignis vocem.*[77]

In this indictment of Homer, Swift skips rapidly through the *Anthroposophia;* from the "*audi ignis vocem*" of Vaughan's title page to the *sphaera pyroplastica,* uniquely Vaughan's

---

[73] Swift read Irenaeus in 1696/7-1697/8. (Sheridan, *op. cit.,* p. 22.)
The sentence in Latin comes from Irenaeus, *contra Haereses,* I, iv, 2. (Guthkelch-Smith, *op. cit.,* p. 352.)
[74] *A Tale of a Tub,* pp. 68-69 (Introduction).
[75] Waite, *Occult Sciences,* p. 184.
[76] Butler, "Hermetic Philosopher," p. 240.
[77] *A Tale of a Tub,* pp. 127-28 (Digression in the Modern Kind).

and ingredient for his magic elixir,[78] to a passing recommendation of Vaughan's to his readers to peruse Sendivogius and Behmen.

These are some of the more interesting details of Swift's satire on occultism in *A Tale of a Tub*; the details can be multiplied.[79] He has blown "the Philosophers Fire with Words of pure Wind";[80] he has drawn "the glorify'd Spirit of the Elixir not out of gross Matter, but the pure incorporeal Hope and Faith of the Credulous."[81] He has been more windy than the philosophers, more illuminated than the *illuminati*, more credulous than the faithful. That he was not always perspicacious in differentiating the streams of occultism, nor even always correct in his details, is not to the point. Swift

[78] See: Vaughan, *Anthroposophia Theomagica*, p. 30: "Rc. Limi coelestis partes decem. Separetur masculus a faeminâ, uterque porro a terrâ suâ, physice tamen et citra omnem violentiam. Separata proportione debitâ harmonicâ et vitali conjunge. Statimque anima descendens a *sphaerâ pyroplasticâ* mortuum suum et relictum corpus amplexu murifico restaurabit. Conjuncta foveantur igne naturali in perfectum matrimonium spiritus et corporis. Procedas artificio vulcanico-magico quousque exaltentur in quintam rotam metaphysicam. Haec est illâ de quâ tot scribillarunt, tam pauci noverunt, Medicina." (Italics mine.)

I doubt that this is jest or parody as Waite suggests in note 1 to p. 30, but secret arcanum. (See: Price, *op. cit., passim;* and Guthkelch-Smith, *op. cit.*, p. 351.)

[79] See, for example, Swift's *"A Panegyrical Essay upon the Number* THREE," announced in the "Treatises Wrote by the Same Author"; and pp. 57, 58 (Introduction), in which Swift announces that the "Panegyrical Essay" "wherein I have by most convincing Proofs, not only reduced the *Senses* and the Elements under its Banner, but brought over several Deserters from its two great Rivals, *SEVEN* and *NINE*" is already in the press. Swift's use of the number three is, if at all, only incidentally satire on Catholicism, since, as an Anglican, he would not wish to satirize the Trinity, although, no doubt, the Catholics endowed it with greater mystery than did the Anglicans.

See also *A Tale of a Tub*, p. 8 (Apology): ". . . *that of Four being much more Cabalistick, and therefore better exposing the pretended Virtue of Numbers, a Superstition there intended to be ridicul'd."*

See too *A Tale of a Tub*, p. 68 (Introduction): "Dr. *Faustus*, penn'd by *Artephius*, an Author *bonae notae*, and an *Adeptus*. . ." and *"Tom Thumb*, whose Author was a *Pythagorean* Philosopher."

[80] Butler, "Hermetic Philosopher," p. 236.
[81] *Ibid.*

was not writing a history of occultism. He was reflecting what he and his contemporaries saw as the black shadows cast by the dark philosophy. He was reducing to the absurd a realm of thought that was easily absurd before reduction. He was ridiculing Vaughan's celestial "Hydro-pyro-magical Art";[82] his precious truths "beyond reasoning [*"extra-intellectum"*]; sensible, practical truths, not mere vagaries and rambles of the brain."[83] But for Swift nothing but the few simple truths of Christianity was *"extra intellectum."* And if it were, how could it be "sensible, practical" truth, anything but "vagaries and rambles of the Brain"? Furthermore, it did not require any great perspicacity in occultism to see how close, despite his orthodox protestations, Vaughan was to gnosticism.[84] Swift knew Irenaeus well. And the occultists were regularly turning up in the questionable company of the Nonconformists. Though the Nonconformists, as a group, were scarcely occultists, Swift's identification of the two in his Aeolist system was a happy one. Through his satire on Aeolism he gently blew the wind of occultism upon the "light" of Nonconformity; for together the wind and the "light" shook and darkened the true light of Reason.

III

In *A Tale of a Tub*, however, "frail man" is not only mad; he is depraved too. His Will is vitiated, just as his Understanding is shaken and obscured. Indeed, the Will could follow the Understanding's methods in error and practice whole systems of depravity no less metaphysical than the systems of madness. Between the overt denial of the spirit in Epicureanism, a system of man's philosophy, and the tacit denial of man's soul in "sartorism" (as, for want of a better term,

[82] Vaughan, *Anthroposophia Theomagica*, p. 62 ("Advertisement to the Reader").

[83] *Ibid.*, p. 9. [84] Price, *op. cit., passim.*

we may call the worship of the Tailor-Deity as expounded in Section II of *A Tale of a Tub*) there is the close correspondence of error, materialism. And if occultism, or Aeolism, exaggerated rather than denied the spirit, its mysticism was no less erroneous, no less a denial of truth than materialism.

Early in *A Tale of a Tub* Swift draws up what appears to be his metaphysical system of man's depravity, the few pages constituting the doctrine and discipline of "sartorism,"[85] the worship of clothes. Basic to Swift's satire on the "sartorists" are: the idea of the universe as a great chain of being, the concept of the correspondence between the macrocosm and the microcosm, and the logical distinction of the "accident," the "fifth universal."

From the Middle Ages to the eighteenth century the universe was pictured as a great chain beginning with God and ending with the least considerable speck in the universe; and it contained a host of intermediate links descending from the most purely spiritual to the most exclusively material. Man, the link about which most attention centered, had within him both the spiritual and material; hence his connections with the celestial and the bestial. The links remained forever discrete, and for one link to attempt to assume the character of a higher link constituted a subversion of the Law of Nature, in man the sin of pride. But within his limitations man could rise or fall, assume his most divine potentiality, or his most bestial.[86]

Add to this picture of the universe as a great chain the concept of the correspondences between man and the universe, the macrocosm and the microcosm,[87] and the universe becomes

[85] Unless otherwise noted, all references to and quotations from the *Tale* in Section III of this chapter are taken from pp. 76-81 (Section II).

[86] See the following:

Arthur O. Lovejoy, " 'Pride' in Eighteenth-Century Thought," *Modern Language Notes*, XXXVI, 31-37 (Jan., 1921).

Arthur O. Lovejoy, *Great Chain of Being*, Cambridge, 1942, pp. 59ff.

[87] Tillyard, *op. cit.*, pp. 63-65.

not only wonderfully linked but wonderfully one. For not only are there parallels between man and the universe, but there are correspondences among the several links, and, indeed, within the crucial link, constituting man, itself.

This chain of parallels, however, essential though it is to Swift's sartorist system, is not crucial. What is crucial is the simple substitution of *clothes* for *man*. This substitution, however, is deceptively simple and by no means fortuitous, for it is a substitution deriving from, and satiric of the most formal logic. Swift's moral indignation at man's depravity lends force to his sartorist system; his logical skill lends it gravity and weight.

Logic was one of the last branches of philosophy to undergo Modernizing. Between the logic of the scholastics and the logic of the Port Royalists only the innovations of Peter Ramus are of great importance.[88] And although the *Port Royal Logic* is in inspiration and method a Cartesian work, *"par excellence,* the logic of Cartesian philosophy,"[89] the authors of the *Logic* did not reject those aspects of Aristotelian logic they found still valid; though even there they reexamined the materials and provided fresh examples to the old precepts. Whether Swift's substitution of *clothes* for *man* in his sartorist system is primarily satirical of Cartesianism or scholasticism is debatable. We know he objected to both.[90] The important fact is that in his sartorist system Swift's basic point derives from the "accident" of Aristotelian[91] logic,

[88] Antoine Arnauld and Pierre Nicole, *Port Royal Logic,* ed. and trans., Thomas Spencer Baynes, London, 1872, "Introduction by the Translator." The *Logic* came out in 1662 and was republished five times in the next twenty years.

[89] *Ibid.,* p. xxix.

[90] For Swift's satire on scholasticism see *A Tale of a Tub,* pp. 83-91 (Section II), *passim,* which deal with the liberties that Peter, "the Scholastick Brother" (p. 89), took with his father's will; see also p. 57 (Introduction), and p. 190 (Section XI).

[91] See: Aristotle, *Organon, or Logical Treatises,* ed. and trans., Octavius Freire Owen, London, 1853, II, 365, and the "Introduction of Porphyry," II, 623-24.

also called the "fifth universal" in the *Port Royal Logic*.

In the chapter devoted to the "five Kinds of Universal Ideas—Genus, Species, Difference, Property, Accident," in the *Port Royal Logic*,[92] the "fifth universal" is defined as that "which we call accident, since it is not *essential* to the thing to which it is attributed; for, if it were, it would be *difference* or *property*." A fuller explanation follows, though it is the example rather than the explanation which is pertinent to our purposes here.[93]

But it must be noted here, as we before said, that when we consider two substances together, we may regard one as a mode of the other. Thus a man dressed may be considered as a whole made up of the man and his dress; but to be dressed is, in relation to the man, only a mode or phase of existence under which we regard him, although the parts of the dress may be themselves substances. And thus *to be clothed* is simply a fifth universal.[94]

Thus a substance (*man*) may be modified not only by a mode (*frail*) to result in an accident (*frail man*), but substances may be modified by other substances to result in accidents; man may be modified by *clothes* to result in the accident *man clothed*. If, then, by a satirical reversal we turn this particular example of the accident *man clothed* around, the result is *clothes manned*, or clothes modified by man;

[92] Arnauld and Nicole, *op. cit.* (Part I, Chap. 7), pp. 50-55. Note that the universal ideas in Aristotle are four, "Difference" being considered part of "Genus."

[93] *Ibid.* p. 55.

See: Charles Kerby-Miller, ed., *Memoirs of the Extraordinary Life, Works, and Discoveries of Martinus Scriblerus*, New Haven, Conn., 1950. This section in the *Port Royal Logic* was called to my attention by Dr. Kerby-Miller's note to VII, 22 of the *Memoirs*.

[94] Arnauld and Nicole, *op. cit.*, p. 55. Note, however, that immediately after this explanation, the authors question the utility of the whole elaborate distinction: "This is more than sufficient touching the five universals, which are treated at such length in the schools. For it is of very little consequence to know that there are genera, species, differences, properties, and accidents; the main thing is to recognize the true genera of things, the true species of each genus, their true differences, their true properties, and the accidents which may be attributed to them."

for in the chop logic which is one of the most useful weapons of the satirist, one accident is as good as another, especially if chop logic happens to describe the facts more accurately than true logic. And now the materials for Swift's sartorist system are complete. Not only is man merely a modification of clothes, all the links of the chain of the universe are clothes modified and the universe is clothes modified, but there are a host of correspondences, all relating to clothes, among the several links of the chain. Upon this formidable structure, we believe, rests Swift's sartorist system, his satire on man's depravity.

First Swift rapidly traces the successive links of the great chain from the Deity to the *primum mobile* to the stars to the earth and to man, emphasizing the fact that each link "invests" the link below it, for the universe is "a large Suit of Cloathes which invests everything." There are many correspondences to be found among the several links, ranging from the Tailor-Deity with his Goose for Ensign to "this Globe of Earth . . . a very compleat and fashionable Dress," its coat made of land, its waistcoat sea, the periwig of the beech, and the white satin doublet worn by the birch.

But Swift's interest in his chain lasts only until he reaches man, for he is a satirist and a moralist, not a metaphysician. Between the microcosm and the macrocosm lie the correspondences that most effectively condemn man.

To conclude from all, what is Man himself but a *Micro-Coat*, or rather a compleat Suit of Cloaths with all its Trimmings? As to his Body, there can be no dispute; but examine even the Acquirements of his Mind, you will find them all contribute in their Order, towards furnishing out an exact Dress: To instance no more; Is not Religion a *Cloak*, Honesty a *Pair of Shoes*, worn out in the Dirt, Self-love a *Surtout*, Vanity a *Shirt*, and Conscience a *Pair of Breeches*, which, tho' a Cover for Lewdness as well as Nastiness, is easily slipt down for the Service of both.

Indeed, as Swift proceeds with his system, the modification

of man becomes so complete, that clothes eventually usurp the functions of man. Even as the Houyhnhnms, they are the "Rational Creatures." "For is it not manifest, that They live, and move, and talk, and perform all other offices of Human Life? Are not Beauty, and Wit, and Mien, and Breeding, their inseparable Properties?" Do they not constitute the difference between a beau, a bishop, and a lord mayor?[95] Are not all the "Faculties of the Mind" clothes?

Embroidery was *Sheer Wit;* *Gold Fringe* was *agreeable Conversation, Gold Lace* was *Repartee,* a huge long *Periwig* was *Humor,* and a *Coat full of Powder* was very good *Raillery.* . . .[96]

And who shall quarrel with Swift for having omitted Reason from the "Faculties of the Mind" of these "Rational Creatures?"

What then is the soul of man, if these are the faculties of his mind? Man is an "Animal compounded of two *Dresses,* the *Natural* and the *Celestial Suit* . . . the Body and the Soul," of which the soul is the "outward, and the Body the inward Cloathing."[97] And rightly so. If man is so perverted that he worships a tailor as his deity, man in his divine attributes no

[95] See: Alexander Pope, *Memoirs of Martinus Scriblerus* (VII), in *Works of Alexander Pope,* ed., William Lisle Bowles, London, 1806, VI, 102-03.

[96] Note in contrast to Swift's virtuosity here a similar satire in which tobacco-boxes rather than clothes indicate the triviality of man. Having no tobacco-boxes, the Ancients were deficient: ". . . for consequently they could have no *tobacco-boxes, tobacco-stoppers,* or *snuff-boxes,* all which are the tests and indications of a man's genius. A large *tobacco-box* shews a man of great and extensive trade and conversation; a small one, well japann'd, shews a gentleman of good-humour, that would avoid smoking for the sake of the ladies; and yet, out of complaisance, does it to oblige the persons he converses with. So, as to *stoppers,* if made of the Royal Oak, it shews *loyalty;* Glastonbury-Thorn, *zeal extraordinary;* a piece of pipe, *humility;* silver, *pride;* black-thorn, *adversity.* . . ." (William King, *Dialogues of the Dead,* pp. 172-73.)

[97] Note Swift's incidental excursion into the traducianism controversy: ". . . that the latter [the body] was *ex traduce;* but the former [the soul] was of daily Creation and Circumfusion." (p. 79)

The supporters of traducianism held that both the body and soul were inherited; their opponents believed that the soul, unlike the body, was created at birth. (Guthkelch-Smith, *op. cit.,* p. 79, n. 3.)

longer exists. No longer does his soul link him to the Creator. Nor has even his body usurped his soul's place. What links man now to his deity, the tailor, is the body of his body, the "outward" dress of his "outward" dress, his clothes. And since clothes officiate for man in the nature of a soul, in effect they become his "inward dress"; and such little real soul as he may have left becomes his least important, outward dress, his body. "By all which it is manifest, that the outward Dress must needs be the Soul." Thus depraved man, depraved for having lost his soul, is properly linked to the macrocosm, the "large *Suit of Cloaths* which *invests* everything." For *clothes* have modified *man so* completely that they have become *man*. Man, having lost his soul, which distinguishes him as man, is no more.[98] Man has become clothes; at least he behaves as if this were so. And to parallel this reorganization of the microcosm, Swift, mindful of the order of philosophy, has reorganized the whole order of the universe to correspond with man.

Sartorism, Swift protests, is neither Ancient nor Modern. He describes it merely to explain the "Circumstances" of his tale, what Peter, Martin, and Jack found when they came to town. But sartorism is actually very Modern indeed. Its milieu is clearly that of contemporary London. Swift offers his system, neither Ancient nor Modern (for it would be inconvenient for a Christian to fight the Ancients-Moderns controversy over depravity), as a body of divinity and philosophy. And Swift's system is truly philosophical in its materials and method. Its thesis is error, in Understanding called madness, in Will depravity. In the system of sartorism, satirical of man's behavior, the continuity is of error, the plenitude is of error, and the unity is of error. Among the sartorists unreason reigns supreme and harmoniously. Rarely does Swift surpass

[98] Perhaps Swift here intended a sly dig at Epicureanism, according to which the soul was an "accident"; both the body and soul were created of the same atoms, according to the Epicureans.

this condemnation of man's depravity, for the gentle tone of sartorism is deceptive; the deepest pessimism pervades its gaiety.[99] Why man is evil does not interest Swift very much. He attempts an explanation but hastily breaks off, impatient and mistrustful of his own, as of others', metaphysics. The moralist need make no explanation; he needs merely to show the facts.[100] Man is positively and negatively depraved, evil and trivial. Whole systems can be drawn up of his depravity, even as man draws up whole systems in his madness, be they theological, scientific, or philosophical systems. Man has divorced himself from his Creator; he has lost his divine soul.

Swift thought with the mind of a philosopher and attacked philosophy. He wrote as dialectically as any metaphysician and attacked metaphysics. He celebrated the power of Reason and attacked man's rationalism. In his immense erudition he attacked intellectualism. In his overwhelming pride as a creature of God he attacked man's pride. Were he not so devout a Christian, he could not have been so militant a moralist; were he not so militant a moralist he could not have been so devastating a satirist of the madness and depravity of "frail man," "sole arbiter of truth, in endless error hurled."

[99] See: T. O. Wedel, "On the Philosophical Background of *Gulliver's Travels*," *Studies in Philology*, XXIII, 434-50 (Oct., 1926): "He [Swift] was a rationalist with no faith in Reason." (p. 449)

[100] See Swift's inconclusive discussion of good and evil in the *Tale*, pp. 157-58 (Section VIII), as it is clarified by the *Mechanical Operation of the Spirit*, pp. 276-78.

3

THE NEW SCIENCE

Lastly, I would address one general admonition to all; that they consider what are the true ends of knowledge, and that they seek it not either for pleasure of the mind, or for contention or for superiority, to others, or for profit, or fame, or power, or any of these inferior things; but for the benefit and use of life; and that they perfect and govern it in charity.

Francis Bacon, *The Great Instauration*[1]

In satiric repudiation of the aims, methods, and results of the new science, *A Tale of a Tub* is dedicated to the universal and utilitarian service of mankind. Swift dedicates it to Prince Posterity as "a faithful Abstract drawn from the Universal Body of all Arts and Sciences, intended wholly for your service and Instruction."[2] *A Tale of a Tub* is "Written for the Universal Improvement of Mankind";[3] for "the peculiar advantage of my dear country, and for the Universal benefit of mankind."[4] " 'Tis a great Ease to my conscience," says Swift, "that I have writ so elaborate and useful a Discourse without one grain of Satyr intermixt." He is pleased to reflect upon "how much emolument this whole Globe of earth is like to Reap by my Labours"; and "the Judicious Reader shall find nothing neglected here, that can be of Use upon any Emergency of Life."[5] Swift recommends that his book be trans-

[1] Bacon, *Great Instauration*, p. 247.
[2] *A Tale of a Tub*, p. 38 (Epistle to Prince Posterity).
[3] *Ibid.*, title page.
[4] *Ibid.*, p. 184 (Section X).
    Note the chauvinistic theme in: Thomas Sprat, *History of the Royal-Society*, London, 1702, pp. 2-3, 421ff.
[5] *Ibid.*, p. 48 (Preface); p. 106 (Section IV); p. 129 (Digression in the Modern Kind).

lated by the foreign academies for "the great Usefulness of the Matter to the Publick."[6] He is confident that *A Tale of a Tub* will be of benefit in its *"Repose* of Mankind." And the several parts of *A Tale of a Tub* are dedicated to universal and utilitarian ends too. Jack discovers an universal medicine, Peter an "Universal *Pickle,"* and a "Sovereign Remedy for the *Worms."* Peter's projects, his *"Puppets* and *Raree-Shows"* are of "great Usefulness." And Wotton's experiments with flies and spittle are sublimely useful. Jack invites punishment for the *"Publick Good"*; and the Aeolists "disembogue" powerful gusts of wind for the "Publick Good." Swift himself satirically recommends Modern systems to help writers to manage "the profoundest and most universal Subjects"; he is busy about *"An Universal Rule of Reason, or Every Man his own Carver"*; and he offers some help towards "an universal System in small portable Volume, of all Things that are to be Known, or Believed, or Imagined, or Practised in Life."[7]

We whom the World is pleased to honor with the title of *Modern Authors*, should never have been able to compass our great Design of an Everlasting Remembrance, and never-dying Fame, if our Endeavours had not been so highly serviceable to the general Good of Mankind. This, *O Universe,* is the Adventurous Attempt of me thy Secretary. . . .[8]

The consistent influence of the doctrine of utility upon experimentalism provides one of the chief bases for Swift's objections to the new science. Bacon's criterion of utility for science was far more than *philanthropia,* a humanitarian solici-

---

[6] *Ibid.,* p. 106 (Section IV).

Note Swift's reference to Chinese, in the light of the fact that Robert Boyle was connected with a large group of Oriental scholars. (Louis Trenchard More, *Life and Works of the Honourable Robert Boyle,* Oxford, 1944, p. 165.)

[7] For the foregoing references to *A Tale of a Tub,* see: pp. 208, 190-91, 109, 107, 109, 128, 129, 153, 148, 130, 125.

[8] *Ibid.,* p. 123 (Digression in the Modern Kind).

tude for mankind; it stemmed from his rejection of authority and especially of the useless subtleties of the schoolmen. For their authority and truth he substituted a more profound authority and truth, one that could be perceived by the senses and checked by experiment. Thus, to him an unsuccessful experiment could be more significant than a successful one, if it were more useful in advancing knowledge. He differentiated between the experiments of light and fruit, and although the experiment of light for him came first, it was always as a potential producer of fruit. "Of all signs there is none more certain or more noble than that taken from fruits."[9] As the Puritans sought simultaneously to glorify God through his works, and to assume, individually, the responsibilities of their salvation, they took great care to invest their Talents fruitfully in godliness, learning, and in earthliness too. Coming upon Bacon's doctrine of utility, they served to strengthen and to popularize it.[10]

Utilitarianism *par excellence* is to be observed in the aims and followers of the Royal Society. Many of its members, like Charles Boyle, insisted upon the usefulness of the experimental philosophy; but the utilitarian ideal was expressed most vividly in Sprat's defense of the Royal Society. He preached an over-all utilitarianism and the necessity for the improvement of mechanical procedures; but more important, he expounded the Royal Society's Baconian hope for a widespread inventory of all knowledge, and as prompt as possible a plan for the application of that knowledge.

Their purpose is, in short, to make Faithful *Records*, of all the Works of *Nature*, or *Art* which, can come within their reach: that so the present Age, and posterity, may be able to put a mark

[9] Bacon, *Novum Organum*, p. 276. See also: *Works of Francis Bacon*, pp. 245, 275, 289, 510.
[10] See the following:
    Merton, *loc. cit.*, *passim*.
    Jones, *Ancients and Moderns*, Chaps. v, ix.
    William Haller, *Rise of Puritanism*, New York, 1938.

on the Errors, which have been strengthned over by long prescription: to restore the Truths, that have long lain neglected: to
push on those which are already known, to more various uses: and
to make the way more passable, to what remains unreveal'd.[11]

To this end he recommended the experimental philosophy
to the nobility and gentry as well as to the commons, not only
to the scientists and those interested in mechanical things,
but to wits and writers. Only through their corporate efforts
would men gain mastery over the world. Thus, incidentally,
would rebellion be reduced. Thus one might even "assist
Nature, our common mother, in her *Operations.*"[12] A more
thoroughgoing utilitarianism than this is hard to imagine,
though we may find it expressed repeatedly in almost every
defense of the new science, and especially in the early *Philosophical Transactions of the Royal Society,* through which
the "Benefit of Mankind," the "Publick Good" recur like
leitmotifs.[13]

Universalism, another aspect of the new science which
Swift satirized in *A Tale of a Tub,* was as Cartesian in its
origins as utilitarianism was Baconian. In hypothesizing the
universality of the laws of science Descartes made his contribution to the idea of Progress. For the authority of the
Ancients Descartes substituted the authority of rational evidence and universal consent.[14] "The grand Secretary of
Nature, the miraculous Des-Cartes," as Glanvil called him,
who had "infinitely out-done all the Philosophers went [*sic*]
before him, in giving a particular and analytical Account of
the Universal *Fabrick,*" had originally planned to call his
Discourse on Method, "The Project of a Universal Science
which can elevate our Nature to its highest *degree of Per-*

[11] Sprat, *op. cit.,* p. 61.
[12] *Ibid.,* pp. 435-36.
[13] See the *Philosophical Transactions of the Royal Society* from 1685
to 1700.
[14] Bury, *op. cit.,* pp. 64-77.

fection."[15] And, unsavory as Cartesianism was to Swift, the word *universal* had other, equally distasteful connotations to him. Scholastic universals probably lingered in his mind to the discredit of scientific universality; Holy Mother Church was traditionally "universal"; and the occultists claimed universalism as their own, whether philosophically or in a practical universal elixir and philosopher's stone.

But basically, orthodox objections to the new science were directed against the faith of the new scientists in their work and in its immediate and potential usefulness. Now that the laws of the universe could be trusted to remain immutable, one could hope to unlock the mystery. The key, the New Philosophy, appeared to be opening the mystery of man, the microcosm.[16] The prospect of unlocking the mystery of Nature, the macrocosm, loomed more than a vision, enticingly bright.[17] Bacon's cautions about method, data, and hypotheses were heeded less in the exposition of the idea of science than in the actual practice of science. Indeed, the faith in and enthusiasm for the idea of science appear to have been considerably greater than the faith in and enthusiasm for the practice of science. If ever the sin of pride (particularly abhorrent to Swift) beset a whole generation, it beset the members of the Royal Society of the Restoration, even as in the next breath they protested their Christian humility.

And this is the highest pitch of *humane reason*; to follow all the

[15] See the following:
Joseph Glanvil, *Vanity of Dogmatizing*, New York, 1931, pp. 211-12.
Bury, *op. cit.*, pp. 66-67.
[16] See: *Phil. Trans.*, No. 123 (March 25, 1676): "This last Consideration, which I shall here mention, aspires to a very high flight of human Reason, as merely human, and searches into one of the greatest depths of Nature, making the fullest discovery of Mankind, as Man is the Microcosme, and *divina particula aurae*; namely to collect and digest into one series, and to bring as into Methodical Volumes, or under one view, the shapes, features, statures, and all outward appearances, and also the intrinsick mentals or Intellectuals of Mankind." (Preface by Henry Oldenburg.)
[17] Sprat, *op. cit.*, p. 436.

links of this chain, till all their secrets are open to our minds; and their works advanc'd or imitated by our hands. This is truly to command the world; to rank all the *varieties*, and *degrees* of things, so orderly one upon another; that standing on the top of them, we may perfectly behold all that are below, and make them all serviceable to the quiet, and peace, and plenty of Man's life. And to this happiness, there can be nothing else added; but that we make a second advantage of this *rising ground*, thereby too look the nearer into heaven; An ambition, which though it was punish'd in the *old World*, by an *universal* Confusion; when it was manag'd with *impiety* and *insolence*: yet, when it is carried on by that *humility* and *innocence*, which can never be separated from true knowledg; when it is design'd not to *brave* the Creator of all things, but to *admire* him the more: it must needs be the utmost perfection of *humane Nature*.[18]

It is this imposing and elaborate edifice of universalism and utilitarianism that Swift seeks to topple by his satire. We have seen the parody in his insistence upon the universality and utilitarianism of *A Tale of a Tub*. He attempted to discredit science even more effectively in *A Tale of a Tub* by subverting the work, as well as the aims, of the Modern scientists, by ridiculing their experiments. To this end he provides illustrations of the work of the new scientists in order to make the reader question not only the validity of their aims but the discrepancy between their aims and their results. How useful and universal is it that rotten wood shines; that the scientists devise remedies for the worms; that they make, or pretend to make voyages to *Terra Australis Incognita?* In *A Tale of a Tub* their medicine is devoted to the clap and the pox, their anatomies prove the outer show prettier than the inner. They lead you to fatuous truths, they are obsessed by air and their words are wind. What, indeed, is "the great

[18] *Ibid.*, pp. 110-11.
   Note, however, that although Sprat, like Bacon, cautions against undue haste in utilizing the new science, the utilitarian note in the *History of the Royal-Society* rings more frequently and more loudly than the note of caution.

usefulness of his [Wotton's] sublime discoveries upon the Subject of Flies and Spittle"?[19]

If one were a gentleman, one had his criterion of utility too, though it was an utility of a kind very different from that of the scientists. In contrast to the pleasantly vague, though avowedly socially conscious "business" of the gentleman, the work of the scientists was considered a-social in its irresponsible lack of utility. So that at the same time that the new science was being impugned for its mean and mechanick utilitarianism, it was also being impugned for its a-social and quixotic lack of utility:

Moderno: *In the meantime, I think I have demonstrated, from the ditches, crevices, tadpoles, spiders, divinity, catterpillars, opticks, maggots, tobacco,* flies, oranges, lemons, cyder, coffee, and linen-

---

[19] For the foregoing references to *A Tale of a Tub,* see: pp. 62, 106, 74, 75, 128, 129.

Note that Boyle reported the phosphorescent glow of rotting wood to the Royal Society, *Phil. Trans.,* No. 31 (Jan. 6, 1667/8): "New Experiments to the number of 16, concerning the Relation between Light and Air (in Shining Wood and Fish). . . ." Sir Nicholas Gimcrack makes a pneumatic engine "to eclipse the light of rotten Wood. . . and putrid Flesh when it becomes lucid." (Thomas Shadwell, *Virtuoso,* [Act v], London, 1676, p. 78.)

See, too, the extensive review of Boyle's "new Experiments Physico-Mechanical, touching the Spring and Weight of the Air," in *Phil. Trans.,* No. 42 (Dec. 14, 1668).

In reference to *Terra Australis,* note that the new science was very much interested in promoting geographical knowledge. (See: Carson S. Duncan, *New Science and English Literature in the Classical Period,* Wisconsin, 1913, p. 22.)

Note that ridicule of the Moderns' interest in insects was widespread. Shadwell's Gimcrack boasts: "'Tis below a Virtuoso to trouble himself with Men and Manners. I study insects. . . ." (Shadwell, *op. cit.* [Act II], p. 49.) Robert Boyle found it necessary on many occasions to justify his interest in "mean" experiments. (See especially: Boyle, *Some Considerations Touching the Usefulness of Experimental Natural Philosophy,* Oxford, 1664-1671.) Sprat emphasized the Royal Society's care "to regard the *least,* and the *plainest* things, and those that may appear at first the most *inconsiderable* as well as the *greatest Curiosities.*" (Sprat, *op. cit.,* p. 90.) The Puritans especially emphasized the fact that even the meanest things were God's handiwork. But as for Wotton, so far as I know he performed no experiments with flies or spittle, though he praised advances in all kinds of natural science.

rags of the Moderns, that "the extent of knowledge is at this time vastly greater than it was in former ages."[20]

And, indeed, the new science was susceptible of both criticisms, utilitarianism and uselessness, depending upon whether it were Baconian or Cartesian. For whereas the Baconians were interested always in the potential fruit of their experiments, the Cartesians, interested in deducing the universal laws of nature, rarely strayed into the laboratory, and when they did, it was, to weigh air "to know what it weighs."[21] Only late in life did Henry More, the Cartesian lend his hand to an experiment.[22] As they were satirized, then, the Baconian was a plebeian, and the Cartesian a pedant, and both were suspected of having a goodly quantity of foolishness in addition.[23]

Before the mid-century, however, the "virtuoso" was both gentleman and scholar. When the virtuosos took over science to replace their waning interest in Antiquities, they were satirized as scientists, not as "virtuosos." They were, primarily, gentlemen devoted to learning. As scientists they took over the Baconian stigma of utilitarianism, and the Cartesian stigma of pedantry, or lack of utility. As dilettante scholars they were scarcely plebeian, and their utility lay in their "business." These, indeed, were the very gentlemen Sprat tried to entice to science.[24] The original "virtuoso," then, not as he was sati-

---

[20] King, *Dialogues of the Dead*, p. 174 (quoting, in part, Wotton's *Reflections*.)

[21] See: Shadwell, *op. cit.* (Act v), p. 78.

[22] Marjorie Hope Nicolson, *Conway Letters*, New Haven, 1930, p. 317.

[23] For the Baconian character of the comic virtuoso, see: C. S. Duncan, "Scientist as a Comic Type," *Modern Philology*, XIV, 287-88 (Sept. 1916).

[24] Walter E. Houghton, Jr., "The English Virtuoso in the Seventeenth Century," *Journal of the History of Ideas*, Part I, III, 51-73 (Jan. 1942); Part II, III, 190-209 (April 1942).

See also the democratic inclusiveness of Sprat, *op. cit.*, pp. 71-72: "All places and corners are now busie and warm about this Work: and we find many *Noble Rarities* to be every day given in, not only by the hands of Learned and profess'd Philosophers; but from the Shops of *Mechanicks;* from the Voyages of *Merchants;* from the Ploughs of *Husbandmen;* from

rized later for his interest in science, was scarcely susceptible of Swift's satire, embodying as he did Swift's own ideal of the humanistically educated gentleman as opposed to the vocationally educated plebeian. At the time the natural philosopher began to be called a virtuoso, real, historical virtuosity begins to decline. Or, the virtuoso as Ancient was replaced by the Modern of the same name. It is the Modern virtuoso, the scientist whom Swift is satirizing in *A Tale of a Tub*. And as "projector" the new scientist had his origins in the past too, as faker and fool.[25] It is significant that Swift retains the outmoded term projector for the scientist, using virtuoso and projector interchangeably, for the most earnest scientists, like Boyle and Sprat, objected to its offensive connotations repeatedly.

It is, then, in a purely current, satirical tradition, without respect to historical or pure definitions, that Swift satirizes the personnel of the new science, the virtuoso-projector, the recipient philosopher whom Shadwell could not differentiate from the emittent ass as the Royal Society transfused their blood.[26] For Shadwell he was an ass; for Swift he was a pedant-plebeian-fool. Given the new science, the virtuoso-projector had a long rope with which to hang himself, a rope

---

the Sports, the Fishponds, the Parks, the Gardens of *Gentlemen;*" See also p. 332.

[25] *Projectour* as used by Jonson in *Devil is an Ass* (1616) has invidious connotations of scheming, cheating, and living by one's wits. By 1692, Charles Boyle, in his *History of Air*, was using *projector* as synonymous with *conjuror*, and he objected to having members of the Royal Society referred to as *projectors*. The word also had alchemical connotations in the "powder of projection" which was being used to achieve transmutation. (*O.E.D.*)

[26] See: Shadwell, *op. cit.* (Act II), pp. 33, 34: ". . . if the bloud of an Ass were transfus'd into a Virtuoso, you would not know the Emittent Ass from the Recipient Philosopher. . . ."

Note also Temple's evaluation of Modern scientific experiments, in *Some Thoughts upon Reviewing the Essay*, pp. 516-17: The Moderns have contributed the universal medicine, the philosophers' stone, transfusions to make old men "gamesome as the lambs from which it [blood] is to be derived," "the art of flying till a man happens to fall down and break his neck," and spittle "to be sold, and very cheap, in the apothecaries shops."

Swift happily provided in the operations of Peter in *A Tale of a Tub*.

As projector and virtuoso Peter is preeminent above his brother Jack in *A Tale of a Tub*.

And then he must be styl'd *Father PETER*; and sometimes, *My Lord PETER*. To support this Grandeur, which he soon began to consider, could not be maintained without a Better *Fonde* than what he was born to; after much thought, he cast about at last, to turn *Projector* and *Virtuoso*, wherein he so well succeeded, that many famous Discoveries, Projects, and Machines which bear great Vogue and Practice at present in the World, are owing entirely to *Lord Peter's* invention.[27]

As a group, the Catholics in England were by no means outstanding in science, any more, indeed, than the Nonconformists were in occultism. Yet the international character of the Royal Society, which Sprat felt it necessary to defend,[28] was, on occasion, feared as the thin end of the wedge of Popery in England. The terminology of the Royal Society had Catholic overtones: the ten secretaries, the Invisible College, the Universal Correspondence; and the experimental philosophers were feared as disguised advocates of a popish plot.[29] But principally, the reason Swift makes Catholic Peter preeminent in science is that he sees in the history of Catholicism a history of experiments upon primitive Christianity, in the doctrine and discipline of the Catholic Church a series of "Discoveries, Projects and Machines" distorting the simple, sufficient truths of the father. Thus some of the most skillful satire on Catholicism in *A Tale of a Tub* is couched in scientific terms. Peter turns projector, he goes mad with "pride, projects

[27] *A Tale of a Tub*, p. 105 (Section IV).
[28] Sprat, *op. cit.*, pp. 64, 65.
[29] See the following:
    Henry Stubbe, *Campanella Reviv'd, or an Enquiry into the History of the Royal Society; whether the Virtuosi there do not persue the Projects of Campanella, for reducing England unto Popery*, London, 1670.
    Isaac D'Israeli, *Quarrels of Authors*, London, 1814, II, 11ff.
    Jones, *Ancients and Moderns*, p. 258.

and knavery," he introduces a whispering office and an universal pickle. The universal pickle, for example, is simultaneously holy water and universal medicine, though the scientists, with a few exceptions like Boyle, were scarcely occultists. Peter's whispering office, immediately satirical of the confessional, recalls a report to the Royal Society of a "whispering place in Gloucester"; it also recalls a suggestion Leibniz made that in some of the houses of his elaborate academies arrangement be made so " 'that the director of the house could hear and see everything said and done without anyone perceiving him, by means of mirrors and openings, something that would be very important for the state, and a species of political confessional,' " a suggestion that to Swift would be reminiscent of Catholic chicanery. And more generally, the whispering office recalls the growing interest in acoustics in the seventeenth century.[30]

Peter also bought a "Large Continent" in *Terra Australis Incognita*, and he "sold the said Continent to other Customers *again*, and *again*, and *again*, and *again* with the same Success,"[31] a sale satirical not only of indulgences and purgatory, but of the geographical interests of the scientists. Again, Swift describes Peter's "Sovereign Remedy for the *Worms* especially those in the *Spleen*":

The Patient was to eat nothing after Supper for three Nights: as soon as he went to Bed, he was carefully to lye on one Side, and when he grew weary, to turn upon the other: He must also duly confine his two Eyes to the same Object; and by no means to break Wind at both Ends together, without manifest Occasion.

[30] See *A Tale of a Tub*, pp. 109, 107, 108 (Section IV).

With the whispering office in the *Tale*, compare Sprat, *op. cit.*, pp. 199ff., and *Phil. Trans.*, No. 156 (Feb. 20, 1683/4). See also: Philip P. Wiener, "Leibniz's Project of a Public Exhibition of Scientific Inventions," *Journal of the History of Ideas*, I, 237, n. 17 (April 1940).

For Swift's interest in acoustics see *A Tale of a Tub*, p. 61 (Introduction), and compare with *Phil. Trans.*, No. 156 (Feb. 20, 1683/4).

[31] *A Tale of a Tub*, p. 107 (Section IV).

These Prescriptions diligently observed, the *Worms* would void insensibly by perspiration ascending thro' the *Brain*.[32]

Obviously the remedy ridicules the ease of securing penances from Holy Mother Church, penances to ease and dispel the gnawings in the conscience of the sinner. Implicit is the satire on the quackery of much seventeenth century medicine. The word sovereign strikes simultaneously at the universal medicine of the occultists and at the quick and easy panaceas for all ills that a utilitarian and over-optimistic science was advocating. And finally, there is the trenchant shock to the mind in the imaginative distance between the agonizing spiritual pains accompanying penance, and the equally agonizing, though scarcely spiritual, pains inflicted by the worms. Least important is the fact that there was scarcely a piece of hack writing of the omnium-gatherum variety, conduct book, complete letter writer, almanac, or omnibus in the seventeenth century which did not include at least one remedy for the worms. Indeed, the eminent Nehemiah Grew's *Musaeum Regalis Societatis* mentioned four![33]

The virtuoso-projector in the company of his kind may be seen in Swift's society or academy satire in *A Tale of a Tub*. Swift requests that the academies at home and abroad take notice of his book since it is of universal benefit to mankind. He accuses the "Societies of *Gresham* and of *Will's*" of being "two *Junior* start-up Societies" threatening the eminence of the Grub Street brotherhood, and he points out their indebtedness to Grub Street "in the Commonwealth of Wit and learning."[34] The inclusion of Will's is a satiric stroke against the scientists as well as against the critics and hacks who haunted it, for the coffee houses had sought added popularity by

[32] *Ibid.*
[33] Nehemiah Grew, *Musaeum Regalis Societatis*, London, 1681, pp. 247, 249, 335, 347.
[34] *A Tale of a Tub*, p. 64 (Introduction).

advertising their collections of natural rarities.[35] But essentially, what Gresham's was to science, Will's was to letters.[36] In *A Tale of a Tub* Gresham's, Grub Street, and Will's are all three of a madness near allied, and it would require "a third indifferent Person . . . to decide which Society each Book, Treatise or Pamphlet do most properly belong to." Thus the scientists take their place among the mountebank wits, and, indeed, along with their brethren in Bedlam.[37]

Not content with these incidental strokes against the societies, Swift sets up his own academy in *A Tale of a Tub*:

It is intended that a large Academy be erected, capable of containing nine thousand seven hundred forty and three Persons; which by modest Computation is reckoned to be pretty near the current Number of *Wits* in this Island. These are to be disposed into the several Schools of this Academy, and there pursue those Studies to which their Genius most inclines them. The Undertaker himself will publish his Proposals with all convenient speed, to which I shall refer the curious Reader for a more particular Account, mentioning at present only a few of the Principal Schools. There is first, a large *Pederastick School,* with *French* and *Italian* Masters. There is also the *Spelling* School, a *very spacious Building*: the School of *Looking Glasses*: The School of *Swearing*: the School of *Criticks*: the School of *Salivation*: the School of *Hobby-Horses*: The School of *Poetry*: The School of *Tops*: The School of *Spleen*: The School of *Gaming*: with many others too tedious to recount. No Person to be admitted Member into any of these Schools, without an Attestation under two sufficient Persons Hands, certifying him to be a *Wit*.[38]

On the face of it Swift's academy project would appear to have very little relation to science. But insofar as it is satirical

---

[35] Duncan, *New Science and English Literature in the Classical Period,* p. 18.

[36] Robert J. Allen, *Clubs of Augustan London,* Cambridge, 1933, pp. 27-32.

[37] *A Tale of a Tub,* pp. 64-65 (Introduction), 181 (Section x).
Note that Swift pays his respects to the Royal College of Physicians too, and lumps all the societies together, even including "*Scotland-Yard* and *Westminster-Hall* and *Guild-Hall*."

[38] *Ibid.,* pp. 41, 42 (Preface).

of the widespread learned society or academy movement in the seventeenth century, it is satirical of Baconian utilitarianism, the advancement of learning for the benefit of man's estate. Actually there were many more proposals for learned academies than were ever put into practice. But whether real or merely proposed; whether political like Harrington's Rota Club; or literary like Edmund Bolton's proposal for an "Academy Royal of King James" or like Dryden's and Sprat's proposals for an academy of letters; or pedagogical like Sir Francis Kynaston's *Musaeum Minervae* or an "universal college" proposed by Comenius; or like Hartlib's, Evelyn's, and Cowley's proposals directly anticipating the Royal Society; the projects and proposals alike, whether independent developments or inspired by France or Italy, were, essentially, as scientific in their motivations as the Royal Society.[39] And much the same desire, to methodize knowledge, to utilize it, and to advance it, inspired them all.

In addition, although some of the schools in Swift's academy project may appear, at first glance, to have been inspired by the most freely associated absurdities, a glance at a similar academy project of Leibniz makes Swift's seem rational and sweetly reasonable in its moderation. Leibniz's project was essentially a museum exhibit, a kind of World's Fair, which, he hoped, would eventually "develop into a self-supporting 'academy' for the encouragement and prosecution of further investigations and inventions." He seems to have intended as much spectacle as science, for in addition to what one might expect to find in a scientific exhibit ("natural" rarities, laboratories, anatomical theaters, telescopes, etc.), Leibniz planned to include " 'representations of charity, and cruelty,' " a fire-eating man, menageries, "Magic Lanterns," horse ballets, aquatic exhibitions, chess games, fire-works, etc. In addition,

[39] See: Harrison Ross Steeves, *Learned Societies and English Literary Scholarship*, New York, 1913, pp. 36-59.

Leibniz planned to surround his exhibition with " 'training Academies and Colleges for youth,' " and with many academies of games, housed throughout the city, and including provisions for cards, dice, and all kinds of gambling. (Swearing, however, was outlawed as disreputable.) Leibniz's project, indeed, was extraordinarily catholic in its variety, and the whole enterprise " 'would some day perhaps be admired by posterity.' "[40] Thus Swift's collation of science and entertainment in his academy project is by no means historically incorrect, for in their attempt to achieve a strong foothold for science, the scientists were by no means averse to popularizing it in whatever ways they could. All for the glory of science and the benefit of man's estate! In time Swift was to propose an academy seriously; nor was he ever opposed to what he considered a true advancement of learning. It was, however, a learning very different from that of the scientists to which he was committed.

The popularization of science, however, was by no means left exclusively to the learned heads of the scientists; Grub Street knew a good thing when it saw it. Exploiting the Baconian ideal, Grub Street developed an interesting phenomenon of pseudo-scientific journalism, the "periodical-project" as it may be called; in part, at least, the common man's *Philosophical Transactions*. The extent to which several of these periodicals are actually "scientific" in character has scarcely been appreciated.[41] The aim of the periodical-project was to

[40] Leibniz's proposal is contained in a fragment, *"Drole de pensee touchant une nouvelle sorte de REPRESENTATIONS,"* 1675. (See Wiener, *loc. cit.*)

It is by no means suggested that Leibniz's fragment was the source for Swift's satirical academy; I merely wish to indicate the current attitudes towards the popularization of science, which prompted Swift's satire.

Dr. Wiener, incidentally, makes the interesting suggestion that connections between science and entertainment warrant a history. (Wiener, *loc. cit.*, p. 234, n. 1.)

[41] A notable exception to this is the unpublished Yale University dissertation by Mabel Phillips (Mrs. Clyde de Vane), *Jonathan Swift's Relation to Science*, 1925, which I was unable to consult before my work was

divert, and, in quick and easy lessons, to instruct the public, by answering its questions, and by providing short-cuts to learning through abstracts, extracts, abridgments, reviews, digests, and bibliographies. The periodical-project answered the questions submitted to it by its public, about religion, love, politics, and anything else, but its preoccupation, like that of the public which questioned it, was with science. It dealt in novelty and New Philosophy, and it managed to combine vulgarity and science in astonishing medley. Its principal begetter was John Dunton, who, no less than Leibniz, saw the infinite possibilities of the popularization of science. Although Dunton's chief interest lay, for his purse's sake, in popularization rather than in science, nevertheless he entertained a lively enthusiasm for science; the outlines of that word, however, were extremely elastic in his mind, and sometimes it was synonymous with novelty. He was, as he said "sufficiently convinc'd, that unless a Man can either *think or perform something out of the old beaten Road,* he'll find nothing but what his Forefathers have found before him."[42] He was, at the moment, congratulating himself on having found a new journalistic angle, but his "authoritative" replies to the scientific (as well as to the other) queries of his public gave that new angle even greater novelty.

On March 17, 1690/91 John Dunton issued the first number of the *Athenian Gazette or Casuistical Mercury* (after the first number the individual issues were called *Athenian Mercury,* the collected numbers *Athenian Gazette*),[43] the

completed. Mrs. de Vane traces the history of the Athenian Society in excellent detail (pp. 74-150), but she does not relate Swift's *Tale* to the Athenians. I rather doubt, too, that so much of the satire on science in Swift's works is directly the result of the publications of the Athenian Society as Mrs. de Vane suggests.

[42] John Dunton, *Life and Errors of John Dunton,* London, 1705, p. 247.
[43] *Athenian Gazette: or Casuistical Mercury, Resolving all the most Nice and Curious Questions Proposed by the Ingenious.* London, printed for John Dunton, 20 vols., 1691-1697.

first publication of the Athenian Society, as Dunton ceremoniously and deceptively called himself and his ever-changing editorial boards; learned society it was none, though obviously Dunton meant to give the impression that it was. In February 1691/92, Charles Gildon, a fellow Grub Streeter, along with Tom Brown and William Pate, the "learned woolen draper," issued the first number of a rival periodical, burlesquing the *Athenian Mercury*, their *London Mercury*, later called the *Lacedemonian Mercury*. Very shortly thereafter, Gildon left the ranks of the burlesquers and joined the burlesqued, and soon he became the *Athenian Mercury's* Sprat, with his *History of the Athenian Society*.[44] In May 1692 Dunton succeeded in putting his rival out of business; whereas the *Athenian Mercury* flourished until 1697.[45] After the demise of the *Athenian Mercury*, the Athenians produced the *Athenian Oracle* (1703-1710), consisting of the "most valuable parts" of the *Athenian Mercury*, its fourth and last volume partially devoted to a reprint of Gildon's *History of the Athenian Society*.[46]

The *Athenian Mercury* designed:

... to satisfy all *ingenious and curious Enquirers* into *Speculations*, Divine, Moral and Natural, *etc.* and to remove those Difficulties and Dissatisfactions, that shame or fear of appearing ridiculous by asking Questions, may cause several Persons to labour under, who have now opportunities of being *resolv'd in any Question* without knowing their Informer.[47]

[44] Charles Gildon, *History of the Athenian Society*, in *Athenian Oracle. Being an Entire Collection of all the Valuable Questions and Answers in the Old Athenian Mercuries*, London, 1728, vol. IV.

[45] For the history of the rivalry between the *Athenian Mercury* and the *London Mercury* (which I have been unable to consult), see: Benjamin Boyce, *Tom Brown of Facetious Memory*, Cambridge, 1939, pp. 38-44.

See also: Harrison Ross Steeves, " 'The Athenian Virtuosi' and 'The Athenian Society,' " *Modern Language Review*, VII, 358-63 (July 1912); Allen, *op. cit.*, pp. 188-92.

[46] For a detailed record of Dunton's periodicals, see: Theodore M. Hatfield, "John Dunton's Periodicals," *Journalism Quarterly*, X, 212ff. (Sept. 1933).

[47] *Athenian Gazette*: or *Casuistical Mercury*, Vol. 1, No. 1 (March 17, 1690/91), "Design of the Work."

The questions submitted ranged from: "*Why* Adam *and* Eve *after the Fall sew'd Figg-leaves together, and made themselves* Aprons?"[48] to a series like the following:

1. *If the Light of the Moon is borrow'd from the Sun, why are they so differing in Complexion?*
2. *Whether there can be any Natural Cause assigned for the Change of the Moon?*
3. *Whether there is a World in the Moon, as some have conceived?*
4. *If there is no World in the Moon, what may we conceive those dark Spots to be which are apparent in it?*
5. *Why the Moons Beams do not convey a warmth as the Sun Beams do?*[49]

The sources of information tapped to answer these questions were highly respectable, if heterogeneous.

'Twere an easy matter to answer those Civil People who abuse at random whomsoever they but suspect *engaged in the* Design; *to answer that Question of theirs,* What Common-place-Books we make use of for filling our Papers? *we might first answer* Common-Sense, *a Book which perhaps they are not much acquainted with, any more than* Civility. *We might add for* Divinity, *we consult* Grotius, Hammond, *the* Criticks, *or whatever* great Names *we could find at the beginning of any* Catalogue; *and that for* Philosophy, *we sometimes read (without being ashamed to own it) the Great* Aristotle, *the Ingenious* Descartes, *the Incomparable Mr.* Boyle, *the Transactions of the* Royal Society, *with those of the Foreign* Virtuoso's. . . .[50]

In addition, each of the first five volumes of the *Athenian Mercury* (the whole encompasses nineteen complete volumes each composed of thirty numbers, with the twentieth volume composed of ten), contained a Supplement:

. . . containing the Transactions and Experiments of the Forreign Virtuoso's: as also, Their Ingenious Conferences upon many *Nice and Curious Questions.* To which is added, An Account of the Design and Scope of most of the Considerable Books *Printed in*

[48] *Ibid.*, Vol. III, No. 17 (Sept. 22, 1691).
[49] *Ibid.*, Vol. XIV, No. 12 (June 30, 1694).
[50] *Ibid.*, Vol. I, "Preface to First Volume," (1691).

all Languages; and of the Quality of the Author, if known. The whole being a *Translation* of what is most Rare and Valuable in the *Paris Journal des Scavans,* the *Acta Eruditorum Lipsiae,* the *Universal Historical Bibliotheque,* and in the New Book Entituled, *Entretiens Serieuses & Galantes, &tc. Published for the Improving of Natural, Moral and Divine Knowledge, &tc.*[51]

As one reads through the welter of Athenianism, one sometimes gets the impression that Dunton and his associates felt that they were latter-day Bacons, who had begotten another Royal Society:

England has the Glory of giving rise to two of the Noblest Designs that the Wit of Man is capable of inventing; and they are the *Royal Society,* for the experimental Improvement of Natural Knowledg; and the *Athenian Society,* for communicating not only that, but all other Sciences to all Men, as well as to both Sexes.[52]

When in August, 1691 Jean Cornado de la Croze published his *Works of the Learned; or an Historical Account and Impartial Judgment of Books newly printed, both foreign and domestic; as also the State of Learning in the world,* John Dunton, zealous for Athenian prerogative, bought him out and continued the periodical from January to May, 1692.[53] Another of Dunton's useful projects for the advancement of learning was the *Young Students Library* which appeared on June 6, 1692. A kind of subsidiary supplement to the *Athenian Mercury,* the *Young Students Library* contained not only an index to the *Mercuries,* but several learned essays, as well as *"Extracts* and *Abridgments* of the most valuable Books Printed in *England,* and in the *Foreign Journals,* From the Year 65. to this present Time."[54]

[51] *Ibid.,* Vol. I, "Supplement" to First Volume, title page, 1691.
[52] Gildon, *op. cit.,* p. 1.
[53] Hatfield, *loc. cit.,* p. 213.
[54] See: *Athenian Gazette: or Casuistical Mercury,* Vol. III, preface: "*PROPOSALS* for Printing a Book Entituled *The Young Students Library,*" 1691.

Such Athenian works were necessary, as Gildon wrote:

... not only for them who cannot go to the Price of the Books themselves, or have no time to peruse so many large Volumes, but also for all the Learned who in a little time may here find the Design of every Book, and some Observation on the Performance, from whence they may frame a Judgment what book to buy, and what not, if they are not fully satisfy'd with it in little; for the chief Force and Matter of most books, lies in a little compass, the ornamental Parts of language generally making up the bulk.[55]

It was Gildon himself, however, who had earlier, in the *London Mercury*, satirized the *Young Students Library* when it was still in prospectus, by asking, "*Whether* the young Student's Library *propos'd by the* Athenians, *be not the cast Common-Place-Book of some Antiquated Pedagogue?*"[56]

Jonathan Swift was not uncritical of Dunton's genius for collecting large numbers of useful volumes, even though he had earlier sent him his "Ode to the Athenian Society" along with an admiring letter, admiration he later repented of.[57]

The ascending Orators [criminals] do not only oblige their Audience in the agreeable Delivery, but the whole World in their *early* Publication of these Speeches; which I look upon as the choicest Treasury of our *British* Eloquence, and whereof I am informed that very worthy Citizen and Bookseller, Mr. *John Dunton,* hath made a faithful and a painful Collection, which he shortly designs to publish in Twelve Volumes in Folio, illustrated with Copper-Plates. A Work highly useful and curious, and altogether worthy of such a Hand.[58]

But principally, Swift's satire on the simplification and vulgari-

---

[55] Gildon, *op. cit.,* p. 57.
[56] Boyce, *op. cit.,* p. 40, quoting Gildon in the *London Mercury.*
[57] Compare Swift's "Ode to the Athenian Society" (*Athenian Gazette: or Casuistical Mercury,* preface to the "Supplement" to Vol. v (March 1691/92), and Swift's letter to the Athenian Society, Feb. 14, 1691/92 (F. Elrington Ball, ed., *Correspondence of Jonathan Swift,* London, 1910, I, 6-8), with his *Public Spirit of the Whigs,* 1714 (Jonathan Swift, *Prose Works,* ed., Temple Scott, London, 1907, v, 315ff.).
[58] *A Tale of a Tub,* p. 59 (Introduction).

zation of learning, his *"New help of Smatterers,* or the *Art of being Deep-learned, and Shallow-read,"* his *"Universal Rule of Reason, or Every Man his own Carver,"*[59] must be related to the kind of popularization of science which was Dunton's province.

The usefulness of *Extracts of Books* need not be displayed by us, since it has been sufficiently evinced by *several Learned* Pens; but is more Evident in the Entertainment they have met with *from the Ingenious in several Languages and Countries.* However, we must beg Pardon if we take the Liberty to say, that the reading of *those Extracts* is the most *Compendious* way to attain to any Perfection in Learning, *since it gives the Substance of a Book in some Hours, (if not minutes) reading* which to find out by Perusing the Book it self will require *not a few days.*[60]

In the same spirit, Swift congratulates himself that:

. . . the Army of the Sciences hath been of late, with a world of Martial Discipline, drawn into its *close Order,* so that a View, or a Muster may be taken of it with abundance of Expedition. For this great Blessing we are wholly indebted to *Systems* and *Abstracts,* in which the *Modern* Fathers of Learning, like prudent Usurers, spent their Sweat for the Ease of Us their Children. For *Labor* is the Seed of *Idleness,* and it is the peculiar Happiness of our Noble Age to gather the *Fruit.*[61]

And again:

What remains therefore, but that our last Recourse must be had to large *Indexes,* and little *Compendiums; Quotations* must be plentifully gathered, and bookt in Alphabet; To this End, tho' Authors need be little consulted, yet *Criticks,* and *Commentators,* and *Lexicons* carefully must. But above all, those judicious Collectors of *bright Parts* and *Flowers,* and *Observanda's,* are to be nicely dwelt on; by some called the *Sieves* and *Boulters* of Learning; tho' it is left undetermined, whether they dealt in *Pearls* or

[59] *Ibid.,* p. 130 (Digression in the Modern Kind).
[60] *Athenian Gazette: or Casuistical Mercury,* Vol. III, preface: "PROPOSALS for Printing a Book Entitled *The Young Students Library,"* 1691.
[61] *A Tale of a Tub,* pp. 145-46 (Digression in Praise of Digressions)

Meal; and consequently, whether we are more to value that which *passed thro',* or what *staid behind.*[62]

Swift's satire on the union of Grub Street and science as they dealt in the *"Sieves* and *Boulters* of Learning," is not directed exclusively against the periodical-project. We shall examine Swift's satire on Richard Bentley in detail in the next chapter. Nevertheless, it is to be noted here that Bentley as critic would not have provoked so much nor so acerb satire had he not been "scientific" in his criticism. It is in satire of Bentley's attempts to methodize and systematize classical learning that he is ridiculed as a Modern systematizer of learning, a dealer in abstracts, indices, and compendiums.

Thus from the satire, in *A Tale of a Tub,* on the utilitarianism and universality of the ideals of the new science, the satire on the experimenters, severally or in society, as pedants, fools, and plebeians, we come back full circle to Swift's satire on the results of the new science, the satire on Grub Street (as Swift so loosely and inclusively used the term) as influenced by science, the advancement of science for the glory of God and the benefit of man's estate, as that advancement is already in progress and soon will be accomplished by the systematization of learning. To a modern reader Swift's satire is scarcely just or perceptive. We can see the universality and utility of seventeenth century science; we are not apt to cringe at the meanness of experiments on spittle; nor to laugh at seventeenth century advancements in acoustics; nor indeed to be puzzled by the connections between universality, utility, and even flies. The learned societies in the seventeenth century scarcely seem crack-brained to us, nor the scientific method in criticism. Nor is seventeenth century science discredited by the periodical-project, any more than twentieth century science is discredited by *Popular Science,* the *Reader's Digest,* with a few columns of advice to the lovelorn thrown in for

[62] *Ibid.,* pp. 147-48 (Digression in Praise of Digressions).

good measure. Swift's satire on science in *A Tale of a Tub* is, therefore, principally of antiquarian interest to us.

The extent to which the new science endangered the *status quo* we have already made clear. As moralist, Swift was justified in his rejection of the new science, bulwark of Modern learning, by the words of Sir William Temple:

. . . ours [Modern learning] leads us to presumption, and vain ostentation of the little we have learned, and makes us think we do, or shall know, not only all natural, but even what we call supernatural things; all in the heavens, as well as upon earth; more than all mortal men have known before our age; and shall know in time as much as angels.[63]

Some of Swift's most light-hearted and happiest satire in *A Tale of a Tub* is his satire on the new science, as if it were not dangerous enough, like Modernity in religion, letters, and philosophy, to earn his savage indignation.

[63] Temple, *Some Thoughts on Reviewing the Essay*, p. 517.

4

THE NEW CRITICISM

HAVING written *The Battle of the Books*, Swift did not need to repeat himself and again to fight the Ancients and Moderns controversy over belles-lettres, though if the aims of *A Tale of a Tub* are to be seen whole, *The Battle of the Books* is to be considered within its framework. Indeed, in avoiding that phase of the controversy, Swift was able to avoid a rather complicated hurdle. *The Battle of the Books*, a mock epic, did not require the painstaking dialectic of a comprehensive satire like *A Tale of a Tub*. Had Swift incorporated it into the *Tale* as a satiric digression on belles-lettres, paralleling the other digressions, he would have had to abandon the satiric rule of *A Tale of a Tub*, last is best; for with very few exceptions the Moderns were not eager to repudiate the Homers; they wished merely to repudiate their authority.[1] For the most part they were ready to award to the Ancients the laurels for genius, especially belletristic genius, provided they were conceded the glory of greater learning. Most of the controversialists in England rather avoided that aspect of the controversy; Temple said poetry required a separate treatment, but he did not supply it; Wotton raced over it

[1] See: Wotton, *Reflections*, pp. 23, 44, 45.
  Dividing belles-lettres into poetry and oratory ("By Orators I understand all those Writers in Prose who took pains to beautifie and adorn their stile."), Wotton hastens over Ancient-Modern superiority in poetry (since very few of even the most militant Moderns claimed superiority in this field), and explains that if Modern orators are worse than the Ancient, it is only because language has deteriorated, one of the few deteriorations he will admit.

with the greatest possible speed;[2] even so firm a believer in progress as Fontenelle admitted that the Ancients had already reached the summit of perfection in poetry.[3] Nor is it probable that the Moderns would have claimed superiority in letters even if they could, bred into their bones from their very youth as the Homers and Virgils were.[4] Nor did Aristotle, Epicurus, Galen, or Pliny have such an early hold upon their imaginations. Thus, it is significant that when Swift satirizes the Moderns' criticism of Homer, he does so in scientific and philosophical rather than in literary terms. Not that there were no Moderns who found fault with Ancient poets, but those faults were summoned as proof that Modern poets were as good as, rarely better than, the Ancient.[5] Swift's satiric rule is scarcely functional here; he cannot, however, resist gloating over the victory that was thereby conceded to the Ancients.

[2] *Ibid.*, Chap III.

Wotton rather evades the whole issue by ascribing reputation in belles-lettres to opinion: "So that, though it may be always debated, who have been the best Orators, or who the best Poets; yet it cannot always be a Matter of Controversie, who have been the greatest *Geometers, Arithmeticians, Astronomers, Musicians, Anatomists, Chymists, Botanists,* or the like." (p. 78.)

See also p. 309: "For these [problems in Natural Philosophy] are things which come under ocular Demonstration, which do not depend upon the Fancies of Men for their Approbation, as Oratory and Poetry very often do."

[3] Bernard Le Bovier de Fontenelle, *Digression Sur Les Anciens et Les Modernes,* in *Oeuvres,* Amsterdam, 1764, IV, 114-31.

[4] See: Wotton, *Reflections,* pp. 22, 23: "So that there is no great Wonder why Men should receive the Writings of the Ancients with so great Respect: For the Distance of Time takes off Envy; and the being accustomed from our Childhood to hear them commended, creates a Reverence."

[5] Rymer almost alone attacks the Ancient poets in England, and Gildon soon repented of his excessively Modern attitude towards poetry. (See: Jones, "Background of the *Battle of the Books,*" pp. 137-42.)

Wotton takes issue with Perrault for finding Modern French poetry superior to the Ancient, and he suggests that Perrault's attitude is the result of excessive translations on the part of the French, and is proof of their "*Sufficiency.*" (See: Wotton, *Reflections,* Chap. IV.)

His [Time's] inveterate Malice is such to the Writings of our Age, that of several Thousands produced yearly from this renowned City, before the next Revolution of the Sun, there is not one to be heard of. . . . But the Concern I have most at Heart, is for our Corporation of *Poets*, from whom I am preparing a Petition to *Your Highness*, to be subscribed, with the Names of one hundred thirty-six of the first Rate, but whose immortal Productions are never likely to reach your Eyes. . . . . The *never-dying* Works of these illustrious Persons, Your *Governour*, Sir, has devoted to unavoidable Death, and *Your Highness* is to be made believe, that our Age has never arrived at the Honor to produce one single Poet.[6]

In *A Tale of a Tub* Swift's satire concerned with Homer[7] is principally a satire against the Moderns' depreciation of Homer, rather than against the Ancients' excessive admiration of Homer. Incidentally he satirizes the Ancients' idolatry of Homer too, but only in passing; for though Swift was an Ancient, he was not a fanatic Ancient, like Thomas Rymer, for example. Had Swift wished to focus his attack upon Ancient idolatry of Homer, he would have satirized his "beauties" and insisted upon Homer as the *arcanum* of all genius and learning; instead, Swift satirizes the "faults" in Homer, in repudiation of the Moderns who felt that if they could break down Homer's overwhelming authority, they could strike a blow against all authority. Like so many Moderns, French and English alike, Swift admitted that Homer was not bad, "a Person not without some Abilities, and for an Ancient of a tolerable Genius"; but had he had the good fortune to have been born a Modern, he would have been incomparably better. In addition, in his satire on Modern anti-Homerism Swift had an opportunity to satirize French chauvinism. Since the Renaissance the French had been searching for a native Homer. Their endless battle of

---

[6] *A Tale of a Tub*, p. 33 (Epistle to Prince Posterity).
[7] Swift's satire on anti-Homerism in *A Tale of a Tub* is contained in pp. 127-30 (Digression in the Modern Kind).

the books over Homer,[8] Swift recapitulates in his own *Battle of the Books*, when he hurls Homer, leader of the Ancient host, against Perrault and Fontenelle.[9] But in *A Tale of a Tub* he changes the focus of his theme, and he finds Homer wanting principally on philosophical and scientific grounds, a focus the French too had used. For it is significant that the defender of Modernity, on any front, even in letters, eventually had to turn to the New Philosophy to buttress his position.

Swift, therefore, willingly concedes Homer the invention of gunpowder and the compass, and the discovery of the circulation of the blood, innovations the Moderns insisted upon so heavily as proof of their superiority.[10] Sir William Temple had found difficulty in depreciating these innovations.[11] Swift is more skillful. Unobtrusively he neatly evades the issue, turning more Modern than the Moderns, who felt moved to apologize for Homer's lack of science and granted him other "beauties" instead. Swift will grant him scientific innovations (of little importance), gunpowder, the compass, and the discovery of the circulation of the blood, and still prove Homer deficient. Because even granted these, Homer is neither a Modern physician nor a physiologist; he has no "compleat Account of the *Spleen*";[12] his *Salivation without*

[8] For the anti-Homerism of the French, see:
Gillot, *op. cit.*, pp. 382ff.
Rigault, *op. cit.*, *passim*.

[9] Jonathan Swift, *Battle of the Books*, in *Tale of a Tub, Battle of the Books, Mechanical Operation of the Spirit*, eds., A. C. Guthkelch and D. Nichol Smith, Oxford, 1920, pp. 245-46.

[10] The invention of gunpowder and the compass were heavily insisted upon as proof of Modern superiority, among others, by Leroy, Cardan, Campanella, Bodin, and Bacon. (See: Bury, *op. cit.*, p. 54, n. 1; Bacon, *Novum Organum*, pp. 292, 300.)

[11] Temple, *Essay*, pp. 469, 472, 473, 476.
Temple, *Some Thoughts Upon Reviewing the Essay*, pp. 493-94.

[12] See: Wotton, *Reflections*, p. 226.
Wotton shows the connections between Modern knowledge about the spleen and the discovery of the circulation of the blood.

Mercury" is ineffective. Nor is Homer a good mechanic; he has no directions for the making of that meanest of little articles, a save-all,[13] "For want of which, if the *Moderns* had not lent their Assistance, we might yet have wandred *in the Dark.*" Nor is Homer a Modern occult philosopher; his *"Opus Magnum* is extreamly poor and deficient"; he has read neither Sendivogius nor Behmen; "He is also quite mistaken about the *Sphaera Pyroplastica.*"[14] Then, turning to the dissenting theme in Modernity, Swift protests that Homer was ignorant of the "Doctrine as well as Discipline of the Church of *England"* (as were the dissenters), nor did he know the "Art of *Political Wagering"* (as did the dissenters but too well).

Swift's satire on anti-Homerism, then, is a satire on Modernity. The skill in it lies in Swift's substitution of scientific, philosophical, and political criteria for literary ones. The literary criteria had been badly overworked by latter day Zoiluses. Swift speaks as a scientific Modern; he grants that Homer has some Modern scientific accomplishments; but he deplores that Homer has not Modernity enough, neither mechanic, occult, nor dissenting.

But although Swift considered the battle over genius already fought and won, outside of *A Tale of a Tub,* it is not to be thought he forgot its counterpart, the battle over Ancient and Modern superiority in learning. The *"Wise Men of* Goatham, *cum Appendice"* proves, according to Swift, the "Learning and Wit" of the Moderns, as opposed to the

[13] Here Homer is satirized not merely as an inadequate virtuoso, but as a poor projector.

See: John Wilson, *Projectors* (Act IV, Sc. 1), in *Dramatic Works,* eds. J. Maidment and W. H. Logan, Edinburgh, 1874, p. 259: Ferdinand, trying to impress the miser Suckdry, says: ". . . if you have ever so much time to spare, read Sir Jeffrey Dropnose, his discourse upon save-alls, or his new method of skinning flints, and perhaps you may not think your time ill spent."

[14] See: Chap. II, Sect. II, *supra.*

"Presumption, the Pride, and the Ignorance" of the Ancients.[15]

So that I can only avow in general to *Your Highness*, that we do abound in Learning and Wit; but to fix upon Particulars, is a Task too slippery for my slender Abilities.[16]

Nevertheless, the Moderns are so learned, the time needs no more instruction:

. . . as Mankind is now disposed, he receives much greater Advantage by being *Diverted* than *Instructed*; . . . in the present universal Empire of Wit and Learning, there seems but little Matter left for *Instruction*. However, in Compliance with a Lesson of Great Age and Authority, I have attempted carrying the Point in all its Heights; and accordingly throughout this Divine Treatise, have skilfully kneaded up both together with a *Layer* of *Utile* and a *Layer* of *Dulce*.[17]

Modern learning is not "in its Cradle" as it was with the Greeks and Romans; the infant has already been "reared, fed, and cloathed" by the "Invention" of the Moderns.[18]

Only very rapidly does Swift ridicule Modern pretensions to Genius in *A Tale of a Tub*: the Genius of the Moderns is "Mignature";[19] it is embodied in *"Tom Durfey*, a Poet of vast Comprehension, an universal Genius, and most profound Learning."[20] But in Criticism, as apart from belles-lettres, the learning of letters rather than its art, the field was wide open for Swift's satire.

I

. . . a *True Critick* is a sort of Mechanick, set up with a Stock

[15] *A Tale of a Tub*, p. 69 (Introduction).

See also Temple's statement that Ancient learning led to humility, and Modern to presumption. (Temple, *Some Thoughts on Reviewing the Essay*, p. 517.)

[16] *A Tale of a Tub*, p. 35 (Epistle to Prince Posterity).

[17] *Ibid.*, p. 124 (Digression in the Modern Kind).

[18] *Ibid.*, p. 144 (Digression in Praise of Digressions).

[19] *Ibid.*, p. 38 (Epistle to Prince Posterity).

[20] *Ibid.*, pp. 36, 37 (Epistle to Prince Posterity).

and Tools for his Trade, at as little Expence as a *Taylor;* and that there is much Analogy between the Utensils and Abilities of both: That the *Taylor's Hell* is the Type of a Critick's *Common-Place-Book,* and his Wit and Learning held forth by the *Goose:* That it requires at least as many of these, to the making up of one Scholar, as of the others to the Composition of a Man: That the Valour of both is equal, and their *Weapons* near of a Size.

"A Digression Concerning Criticks"

The nature and function of criticism, as embodied in Swift's criticomastix in *A Tale of a Tub,* "A Digression Concerning Criticks," constitutes the material for Swift's most ingenious satire on the critical canons of the Moderns. Swift's satirical symbol for his condemnation of Modern criticism is the tailor-critic, even as his satirical symbol for his condemnation of Modern depravity is the tailor-deity. The pervasiveness of the mechanick image for the Modern critic throughout the Phalaris Controversy—in Temple, Boyle, and Atterbury[21]—is significant. It is significant of the fact that Swift's criticomastix is immediately rooted in the literature of the Phalaris Controversy; it is more deeply significant of Swift's primary objections to the Modern critic, that he was neither

[21] a) ". . . an Ill Critic, who sets up the Trade without a Stock to manage it, must be perpetually on the Plunder." (Charles Boyle, *Dr. Bentley's Dissertations . . . Examin'd,* p. 226).

b) *"There are . . . in Learning, as in War, a sort of Inferiour and Subaltern Officers; Men, who seem made only for Registers and Magazines to store up the Productions of better writers. . . . These are They, who among All the Little Men, and Some Great Ones, go for Scholars: but among the Wise and Sensible part of Mankind, for* Pedants. (*Ibid.,* p. 99, citing La Bruyère.)

c) "This [recovering whole books] was as much above any thing our little Pedants pretend to as building the Church of St. *Paul's* is a greater work than mending a few Panels in the Windows of it." (Atterbury, *op. cit.,* p. 134.)

d) "I must confess that the critics are a race of Scholars I am very little acquainted with; having always esteemed them but like brokers, who, having no stock of their own, set up a trade with that of other men; buying here and selling there, and commonly abusing both sides, to make out a little paltry gain, either of money or of credit, for themselves, and care not at whose cost." (Temple, *Some Thoughts Upon Reviewing the Essay,* p. 507.)

scholar nor gentleman, but plebeian and pedant. And, unquestionably, Swift's tailor-critic is the satiric prototype of
Richard Bentley, the Modern, scientific critic.

One of the chief objections to Bentley by his antagonists
in the Phalaris Controversy was that the "library-keeper"
had presumed to correct Sir William Temple, that Bentley had
ostensibly been rude to a sprig of the nobility, Charles Boyle.[22]
The gentleman born and bred was to be careful of the repu-
tations of people in high places; he was to avoid contention;
he was to occupy himself with socially important affairs, to
be a "man of business"; indeed, he was not even to embrace
the homely similitude or to use otherwise "unrefined" language. He was to be a man of wit and of taste, of learning,
business, manners, politeness, civility, modesty.[23] And so
close was the ideal of the scholar to the ideal of the gentleman,
that it is sometimes difficult to distinguish the components
of scholarship from those of gentility. Indeed, the two ideals
were inextricably interwoven in the Renaissance, in the type
of the pure virtuoso.[24]

The pedant, the antithesis of the gentleman-scholar, lacks
wit and taste. Swift's hatred of pedantry is well known; and,
no doubt, that hatred directly determined his insistence upon
taste.[25] Thus, somewhat nervously, Swift entrusts *A Tale of*

[22] Boyle, *Dr. Bentley's Dissertations . . . Examin'd*, pp. 91ff.: ". . .
anybody that reads Dr. Bentley would easily guess, that he is not a *Man of
Business*. And not being a Man of Business, but a *Library-Keeper*, it is not
overmodestly done of him, to oppose his Judgment and Taste in this case
to that of *Sir William Temple;* who is certainly a Man of Business and
knows more of these things. . . ."

See also pp. 199ff.

[23] Note Swift's insistence on politeness as the mark of a gentleman and a
scholar throughout the *Tale*, and compare it with Atterbury's preface to
the *Short Review*, and with Boyle's *Dr. Bentley's Dissertations. . . Examin'd*
throughout.

It is to be noted, however, that Bentley leveled exactly the same charges
of vanity and impoliteness against his opponents, though he did not question
their gentility.

[24] Houghton, *loc. cit., passim.*

[25] Quintana, *op. cit.,* p. 50.

a Tub to the "men of taste"; they have praised it; the "men of taste," his peers, will not misinterpret the intentions of his satire.[26] Nor was wit unrelated to caste at the time Swift wrote *A Tale of a Tub*. The rising bourgeoisie at the end of the century began to demand and to create a polite literature in which the *sense*, the useful and earnest, displaced the more delightful emphasis on thought and style, the *wit* of the aristocracy.[27] Thus Bentley's lack of wit, even more than his lack of taste, was a source of endless delight to the Christ Church Wits. Either they found that such wit as he had was false, or they accused him of having none at all. Swift too satirizes Bentley and Wotton, as proper "yokemates" in false wit, and he ridicules their banter, their railleries and rallyings, their "happy Turns and Flowings."[28] The pedant, then, having neither wit nor taste, is no gentleman; he has no manners. He is interested in vain and useless knowledge; he is proud and ostentatious of the most insignificant details he has amassed, and he exaggerates their importance. He abuses the language.[29]

But primarily, in the Phalaris Controversy and in *A Tale of a Tub* the pedant critic is the rifler of his betters, the systematizer, the lexicographer, the maker of indices, florilegias, and observandas; when he does not create these "Utensils,"

[26] For Swift's references to taste in the *Tale*, see: Apology, *passim*, and pp. 48, 92, 143.

[27] Robert M. Krapp, "Wit and Sense in Seventeenth Century English Literature," *Science and Society*, x, 80-92 (Winter, 1946).

[28] *A Tale of a Tub*, pp. 37-38 (Epistle to Prince Posterity); p. 128 (Digression in the Modern Kind).

[29] *Ibid.*, p. 124 (Digression in the Modern Kind).

Bentley used the word *oscitation* which Swift here ridicules. Bentley was also ridiculed for his use of the homely similitude and for his colloquial expressions: "Why does Dr. *Bentley*, an Englishman, write a New Language, which no Englishman before ever wrote or spoke? How comes his Speech neither to be that of the Learned, nor that of his Countrey? but a mix'd particolour'd Dialect, form'd out of both?" (Boyle, *Dr. Bentley's Dissertations. . . Examin'd*, p. 185.)

See also: *A Tale of a Tub*, p. 19 (Apology); tne attack here is on Wotton, but it applies to Bentley too.

at least he employs them for his knowledge. He is a thing of shreds and patches, his sum of knowledge a tailor's hell of commonplace book gleanings. The ideal of which Swift's tailor-critic is the subversion, the gentleman-scholar critic, is most clearly characterized by Charles Boyle, from whom, indeed, Swift borrowed some of his sharpest weapons against Bentley:

> A good Critick distinguishes himself always by the Choice of his subject; it is some Point of importance, and worth determining: an Ill One is ever busied in things of no manner of Use nor Consequence; and yet is as full of Himself, and his Performances, as if the Commonwealth could not subsist without 'em.
> A Good Critick is Modest and Decent in his Censures. . . speaks with Respect of those he differs from; never takes a pleasure in insulting over their Mistakes, or lessening their Reputations. . . .
> *Salmasius and Scaliger* . . . were all Gall, and Pride, and Pedantry. . . .
> A Good Critick is rich in his own Store. . . an Ill Critick. . . must be perpetually upon the Plunder. . . .
> To compleat the Character of a Critick, it is requisite, that he should write well in that Way he pretends to censure. . . . but *Some now alive* have ventur'd to Criticize upon the Performances of very fine pens, while they themselves had the worst in the world; and have set up for Judges of Good Writing by a Tast form'd upon the Opinions, and in a Style drawn from the Expressions of Modern Prefaces and Comments.[30]

It is simple enough to see the social implications in the ideal of the scholar-gentleman critic. It is much more important, however, to see the implicit attack on Baconian systematization and utilitarianism in the character of the pedant-plebeian critic.

In the history of letters Bentley is preeminent as a pioneer in the application of the new scientific method to literary criticism; it is primarily for this reason, in addition to his

[30] Boyle, *Dr. Bentley's Dissertations. . . Examin'd*, pp. 224-27.

sympathy for the Royal Society, that he was attacked as a Modern, ardent and effective classicist though he was. Classical literature in his time was holy ground; like revealed truth it provoked piety and awe, which are unfriendly to scientific analysis. For his own use Bentley constructed some elementary tools of historical research, without which, he saw, many of the most puzzling problems in classical literature could never be solved; he provided himself with lists and indices; he constructed a rudimentary hexapla; he proposed to compile a dictionary. In his writings he digressed endlessly, supplying variant readings, making corrections in corrupt texts, providing historical, geographical, and even anthropological explanations and data. In the face of his tremendous erudition and pioneering ingenuity, many of his contemporaries were completely befuddled; they failed not only to give him due credit, but they failed even to understand what he was talking about, and they assumed that so did he.[31] The Christ Church Wits were inordinately mirthful at Bentley's expense. They saw in his scientific approach to the history of literature mere thievery, pillaging, and a tacit admission of his own poverty. As in the work of the scientists, they mistook Bentley's means for his end, and saw only the meaningless tool in place of the potential finished product it was to effect. He became a figure of fun, and through their ridicule Bentley retained forever after the reputation, among his contemporaries, of being a mere index maker, a lexicographer.

Bentivoglio has vindicated the worth and honour of all Dictionaries. . . . he has "restored me" in "ten thousand places," and "collated me" with all the manuscripts in the world but those of the King of Poland's Library. Methinks you do not seem so pleased with the news as you ought to be. Are you not concerned

---

[31] See the following:
    R. C. Jebb, *Bentley*, New York, 1889.
    Phillips, *op. cit.*, pp. 191ff.

for the wit, reputation, and honour, of one that can write a Dictionary? . . . What! no wit, breeding, complaisance, politicks, knowledge of men and manners, to be learned out of Dictionaries?[32]

Thus when Swift assailed the "True" Modern critic in his "Digression concerning Criticks," and elsewhere in *A Tale of a Tub*, he accused him of having no wit, learning, or manners; "Before one can commence a *True Critick*, it will cost a man all the good Qualities of his Mind." He accused him of pilfering from the great, of being ungrateful to his sources, of having no manliness, of being mean and contentious,[33] of being a thing of prefaces and appendices.[34] And he defined the pedant as a man "without all Taste and Refinement, little versed in the Course of *present* affairs. . . ."[35] And thus emerged Swift's mechanick critic, not the ninth part of a scholar, and certainly no part of a gentleman. When Swift thus characterized his "True Critick," in less polemical language though to more devastating effect, he was satirizing Modern critics on the same grounds that the Christ Church Wits satirized Richard Bentley. And whether they knew it or not, they were all satirizing Bentley as a scientific critic.

[32] King, *Dialogues of the Dead*, p. 156.
[33] *A Tale of a Tub*, p. 19 (Apology).
See also p. 10 (Apology): ". . . *the Earl of* Orrery's *Remarks will be read with Delight when the Dissertation he exposes will neither be sought nor found. . . .*"
[34] *Ibid.*, p. 54 (Preface); p. 131 (Digression in the Modern Kind).
[35] *Ibid.*, p. 35 (Epistle to Prince Posterity).
See also: King, *Dialogues of the Dead*, pp. 145, 153: "Why, some are of your opinion, that indeed Bentivoglio is a *heavy* Writer; and say farther, 'That he is too bulky and too tedious; that he argues upon trifles with too great gravity, and manages serious things with as much lightness; that he has pillag'd Authors to gain a reputation, but has so managed his contrivance that he has lost his end.' In short, there are mighty disputations whether he has least wit, judgement, or good-manners. . . . Our great Scholars are so much taken up with such fellows as this Hercules, Hyllus the Wrestler, Cleanthes the Cuffer, Phalaris and Xerxes the Man-Eaters, that they never mind 'my actions,' nor several other of their own countrymens."

II

The mechanick-critic, however, is only incidental to Swift's main business in "A Digression Concerning Criticks"; that is to prove, satirically, that Modern criticism is greater than Ancient criticism. To achieve this he defines, at great length, the "True Critick."

From the ranks of critics Swift first carefully excludes the Farnabys and Minelliuses, whose business is not *"to point out the Beauties and Faults,"* at which they are notoriously inept; they are the critics who come to their craft without being called; theirs, incidentally, is the category to which he relegates the critics of *A Tale of a Tub*.[36] There are, however, two kinds of valid critics, first: "the Restorers of Antient Learning from the Worms, and Graves, and Dust of Manuscripts"; but more important "such Persons as invented or drew up Rules for themselves and the World, by observing which, a careful Reader might be able to pronounce upon the production of the *Learned*, form his Taste to a True Relish of the *Sublime* and the *Admirable*, and divide every Beauty of Matter or of Style from the Corruption that Apes it."[37]

Nor was the critic's function to revel in faults, any more than a man walking in Edinburgh's streets reveled in the filth, but strove to keep his skirts clean; any more, indeed, than a judge "who should take up a Resolution to hang all Men that came before him upon a Tryal." It is to be noted, however, that these two kinds of valid critics are no more, "the Races of these two have been for some Ages utterly extinct."

[36] *A Tale of a Tub*, p. 15 (Apology).
Note that in actual fact the Minelliuses and Farnabys wrote the observandas and florilegias, the "bright parts," and "flowers" which Swift seems to lay at the door of the scientific critics.
[37] See the following:
Atterbury, *op. cit.*, p. 4.
Temple, *Some Thoughts on Reviewing the Essay*, pp. 507ff.

The abuses in Modern criticism are, however, best seen in Swift's satiric delineation of the "Third and Noblest Sort," the "True," the Modern critic.

Every *True Critick* is a Hero born, descending in a direct Line from a Celestial Stem, by *Momus* and *Hybris*, who begat *Zoilus*, who begat *Tigellius*, who begat *Etcaetera* the Elder, who begat *B--tly*, and *Rym-r*, and *W-tton*, and *Perrault*, and *Dennis*, who begat *Etcaetera* the Younger.

It need cause no surprise to find the True Critick of Ancient vintage, for he stems from the worst of Antiquity; close kin to Satan, offspring of chaos and dark night, the True Critick is begotten of primeval night (or carping faultfinding) and pride. This hero critic is by definition a *"Discoverer and Collector of Writers Faults,"* which he drags out, multiplies, and emulates.[38] In allying the Modern hero critic with the worst of Antiquity Swift applied his satiric rule to marvelous advantage. To show the illustrious nature of the "True" French and English critics, he disputed the contention of the Moderns that they were unrelated to so "Antient and Illustrious" a heritage as that which began with Momus and Hybris, a heritage "by which they pretend to prove, that the very Art of *Criticism*, as now exercised, and by me explained, is wholly *Modern*." It is as if Swift had said to the Moderns, "If you will be as great as the Ancients, even greater through your progress, the heirs of all your ancestors, the dwarfs taller for being perched upon the shoulders of the giant—then look at your heritage. The particular giant on whose shoulders you sit is not of the race of true giants; though you, indeed, are truly dwarfs."

This is Swift's proof of the Ancient lineage of the True,

[38] It is interesting to note here that like many other classicists who, though devoted to the rules, nevertheless fought an intramural squabble over faults *versus* beauties, Swift leaned towards the school of taste, which emphasized the indication of beauties rather than of faults as the critic's chief function. (See: J. E. Spingarn, ed., *Critical Essays of the Seventeenth Century*, Oxford, 1908-1909, I, xcviii-xcix.)

Modern critics, derived, ironically enough, from his perusal of "Our Noble *Moderns;* whose most edifying Volumes I turn indefatigably over Night and Day, for the Improvement of my Mind, and the good of my Country": first, "True" critics point out the weaknesses of the Ancients, and thus their connections with Hybris, Zoilus, and Tigellius; second, that Modern critics:

. . . have proved beyond contradiction, that the very finest Things, delivered of old, have been long since invented, and brought to Light by much later Pens, and that the noblest Discoveries those *Antients* ever made, of Art or of Nature, have all been produced by the transcending Genius of the present Age.

Swift's second proof of the Ancient lineage of Modern critics is an ingenious and subtle satire on Bentley, who, his critics claimed, found in the Ancients what was not worth finding, and sometimes, indeed, what was never in them.[39]

Swift's third proof of the Ancient lineage of Modern critics, that the Ancients knew the type of the True Modern critic, but out of caution described him in hieroglyph, is an obvious parody on Bentley's controversial and critical style as well as of his critical technique.

It well deserves considering, that these *Antient* Writers in treating Enigmatically upon the Subject, have generally fixed upon the very *same Hieroglyph,* varying only the Story according to their Affections or their Wit. For first: *Pausanias* is of Opinion, that the Perfection of Writing correct was entirely owing to the In-stitution of *Criticks;* and, that he can possibly mean no other than the *True Critick,* is, I think, manifest enough from the following Description. He says, *They were a Race of Men, who delighted to nibble at the Superfluities, and Excrescencies of Books; which the Learned at length observing, took Warning of their own Accord, to lop the Luxuriant,* the *Rotten,* the *Dead,* the *Sapless,* and the *Overgrown Branches from their Works.* But now, all this he cunningly shades under the following Allegory; that the Naupalians in Argia, *learned the Art of pruning their Vines, by*

<hr>

[39] See: Phillips, *op. cit.,* p. 227.

observing, that when an ASS had browsed upon one of them, it thrived the better, and bore fairer Fruit. But *Herodatus* holding the very same *Hieroglyph,* speaks much plainer, and almost *in terminis.* He hath been so bold as to tax the *True Criticks,* of Ignorance and Malice; telling us openly, for I think nothing can be plainer, that *in the Western Part of* Libya, *there were* ASSES *with* HORNS: Upon which Relation *Ctesias* yet refines, mentioning the very same Animal about *India,* adding, *That whereas all other* ASSES *wanted a* Gall, *these horned ones were so redundant in that Part, that their Flesh was not to be eaten because of its extream* Bitterness.

NOW, the Reason why those Antient Writers treated this Subject only by Types and Figures, was, because they durst not make open Attacks against a Party so Potent and so Terrible, as the *Criticks* of those Ages were: whose very Voice was so Dreadful, that a Legion of Authors would tremble, and drop their Pens at the Sound; For so Herodatus tells us expressly in another Place, how *a vast Army* of Scythians *was put to flight in a Panick Terror, by the Braying of an* ASS. From hence it is conjectured by certain profound *Philologers,* that the great Awe and Reverence paid to a *True Critick,* by the Writers of *Britain,* have been derived to Us, from those our *Scythian* Ancestors.

Our quotation of this passage could well be continued for the rest of Swift's paragraph and the one following it, as he proceeds to summon further proof of his point from Diodorus, Lucretius, and Ctesias. Nor would we have quoted at such length if this passage from Swift's "Digression concerning Criticks" were not of such astonishing virtuosity. Only the most careless reader could suppose that this is parody of the Ancients. Swift's contemporaries, and especially those who followed the Phalaris Controversy, could see, much better than we, how obviously this is a parody on Bentley. A glance at almost any page of Bentley's *Epistles of Phalaris* will indicate with what success Swift has caught Bentley's manner to the life: his collation of abstruse sources, his digressive interpolations, his assurance, and, above all, his detailed and accomplished erudition down to its frequently absurd details.

Nor can we fail to admire Swift's ability to erect so elaborate, if deliberately tottering, a structure to prove his own point, that Modern critics are of an accomplished and varied asininity. Had Swift merely parodied Bentley's critical manner so aptly, it were success enough. But to be able to parody Bentley's manner, and simultaneously through the matter of the parody to prove him an ass, all the while competing with him in his own specialty, classical criticism (and Swift scarcely errs in a detail), proves Swift an even greater parodist than he has been acknowledged. Furthermore, in Swift's use of the ass as hieroglyph, a *leitmotif* even more pervasive in *The Mechanical Operation of the Spirit* than in *A Tale of a Tub*, we see his parody on the academic Billingsgate of the Phalaris Controversy. The ass assumes heroic proportions in the Bentley-Boyle part of that controversy; and in the mixture of asininity and erudition in the following passage, we may see again how brilliant Swift's parody is:

And *by the help*, he [Boyle] says, *of a Greek proverb, I call him downright Ass* (p. 11). After I had censured a passage of Mr. B's translation that has no affinity with the original, *This puts me in mind,* said I, *of the old Greek proverb, that Leucon carries one thing, and his Ass quite another.* Where the *Ass* is manifestly spoken of the *Sophist,* whom I had before represented as *an Ass under a Lion's skin.* And if Mr. B has such a dearness for his Phalaris, that he'll change places with him there, how can I help it? I can only protest that I put him into Leucon's place; and if he will needs compliment himself out of it, *I must leave the two friends to the pleasure of their mutual civilities* (p. 25).[40]

[40] Richard Bentley, *op. cit.* (Vols. I and part of II of Dyce's edition contain the so-called "Second Dissertation" 1699, "with an answer to the Objections of the Honourable Charles Boyle." The latter half of Vol. II contains the first, 1697, edition of the *Dissertations,* as it was originally appended to the second, 1697, edition of Wotton's *Reflections.*

The passage quoted in the text comes from Bentley's "Preface" to the "Second Dissertation," I, xlvii-xlviii.

See also I, 204-24 in which the Zancleans are summoned as proof of the spuriousness of the *Epistles of Phalaris;* Bentley cites Herodatus, Pausanias, and Diodorus in proof of his point, in very much the same manner that Swift does in his parody.

And again:

> . . . he [Boyle] says, I compare him with *Lucian's Ass;* which, were it true, would be no *coarse compliment,* but a very *obliging* one. For *Lucian's Ass* was a very intelligent and ingenious Ass, and had more sense than any of his Riders: he was no other than Lucian himself in the shape of an Ass, and had a better talent at kicking and bantering than ever the Examiner will have, though it seems to be his chief one. Let the reader too observe by the way, that Mr. B. in this place has it, *Lucian's Ass;* but in another he cites it truly, *Leucon's Ass. . . .*[41]

Swift parodied Bentley elsewhere in *A Tale of a Tub,*[42] but never to such excellent satiric effect as in the "Digression Concerning Criticks," where Bentley is the prototype of the "True" Modern critic, the pedant-plebeian, the mechanick and scientist, the ass of the Ancient heritage of asses.

It has been justly noted that Swift's aesthetic principles "were but an extension of his moral theories."[43] Swift's aesthetic principles emerge only negatively and incidentally in *A Tale of a Tub,* for the satirist is always negative though a positive purpose impels his satire. They emerge sufficiently, however, to indicate that Swift's aesthetic and critical principles were parts of a harmonious whole, a consistently Ancient, neoclassical creed.

This, then, completes the survey of Swift's satiric themes in *A Tale of a Tub,* of his moralistic attack upon the new

[41] *Ibid.,* I, liii.

See also *A Tale of a Tub,* p. 184 (Section x): "And if it should so happen, that the *Furniture of an Ass* be clapt, by a Mistake upon my Back, that he will immediately please, in the Prescence of the World, to lighten me of the Burthen, and take it home to *his own house,* till the *true Beast* thinks fit to call for it."

[42] See: Phillips, *op. cit.,* pp. 227-37 for an excellent account of the details of the parody on Bentley in *A Tale of a Tub.* I think perhaps Dr. Phillips carries her point a little far; nevertheless, as she proves, many of the Latin words, hard words, philological derivations, and citations of lost authors in the *Tale* are undoubtedly parody of Bentley.

[43] Quintana, *op. cit.,* p. 62.

learning; the madman has invaded philosophy, science has been invaded by the pedant-plebeian-fool, who, in turn, has lent his character and his method, his plebeianism and his pedantry, to criticism.

5

THE SATIRIC PATTERN

THROUGH the analysis thus far of the themes of Swift's satire in *A Tale of a Tub* the larger part of the purpose in this study has been the reconstruction of the contemporary intellectual milieu, in philosophy, science, and criticism, as Swift, the moralist of Ancient persuasion, reflected it in his satire on learning in *A Tale of a Tub*. There remains the explanation of the vehicle of Swift's satire on the abuses in contemporary religion and learning, the form of *A Tale of a Tub*. Insofar as any artistic structure serves to baffle its audience, to confuse the theme, for the expression of which the structure was adopted or created, that structure may be considered a failure. Certainly the critical history of *A Tale of a Tub* supports the conclusion that the structure of *A Tale of a Tub* is a failure, that it not only fails to clarify Swift's theme but goes far to obfuscate it. And yet at the same time that *A Tale of a Tub* has been condemned as baffling, confusing, chaotic, or formless, its detractors have been uneasily insistent that it is nevertheless a very great book. It is our contention that such failure as exists in *A Tale of a Tub* is the reader's, not Swift's.

The apparent disorder of *A Tale of a Tub* is actually the most carefully articulated order, disguised as disorder, for a purpose. The form of *A Tale of a Tub* is a sweeping parody which determines the limits and sequence of the individual sections of *A Tale of a Tub*, and which is itself determined by the Grub Street formlessness that Swift intended to satirize through his structure. *A Tale of a Tub* is neither erratic nor fortuitous in structure; its carefully integrated pattern is arranged for the most thoroughgoing condemnation of the formlessness of Modern writing. Swift's structure, therefore, provides a natural setting for the development of his satiric themes, the benighted state of Modern philosophy, science, and criticism, and, as parody, is in itself a tacit satire on the forms in which the Modern writers couched their Modern philosophy, science, and criticism.[1] Together, matter and method, they constituted the *status quo* in learning. Swift's virtuosity in this two-fold attack on Modern learning is extraordinary. He becomes a Modern, he writes like any Grub Street brother, he pleads the Moderns' cause, he extols the Modern learning, all in the "Modern Kind" of writing.

As the parody implicit in the structure of *A Tale of a Tub*, is examined in detail two points must be kept in mind: first, that exaggeration is the legitimate weapon of the satirist; and second, that Swift was writing a parody not of a man, nor even of several men, but of a manner of many men. If we look to any single contemporary writer for a tale in which, simultaneously, the digressions outweigh his tale proper, in which his prefatory materials weigh half as much again as his tale, in which his formlessness is ingenuously underlined by alternating sections of tale and digression, not to mention many of the other details of Swift's parody which we shall encounter later, we shall probably be disappointed and our appreciation of the power of Swift's satire proportionately decreased. But we can find the digression developed to an extraordinary extent and ingenuousness in Burton,[2] we can

[1] Since he used allegory to satirize abuses in religion, Swift had an easier task there than in his satire on abuses in learning. Allegory automatically allows for satire on manner as well as on matter. Thus when Jack expounds his predestinarian doctrine, he can simultaneously assume the style of the dissenting preacher: "For O ye Eyes, ye blind Guides; miserable Guardians are Ye of our frail Noses. . . ." (*A Tale of a Tub*, pp. 193ff. Section XI.)

[2] It appears very doubtful to me that Swift had Robert Burton particularly in mind when he wrote the *Tale*. Granted their digressions in common, there is very little other reason to suppose that Swift is satirizing Burton, and a good deal of reason to think that he is satirizing what he terms Grub

see how many of Dryden's prefaces are much more significant than the tales they preface,[3] and we know how hosts of contemporary writers, like Bentley,[4] interrupted themselves with digressions, apologetically, but for pages on end. It is the tendency, the composite of Modern writing that Swift parodies in his structure of *A Tale of a Tub*. And, as we shall see, his exaggeration is not frequently gross, nor is his composite parody inapplicable in great detail in specific instances.

That composite manner of many men which Swift satirizes in *A Tale of a Tub* is the manner of what he calls Grub Street. The fine line of demarcation which according to Swift separated the hackney writer from his legitimate colleagues is not drawn very clearly in the *Tale*. His relegation of Dryden, Wotton, Bentley, D'Urfey, Dennis, Blackmore, and L'Estrange to the purlieus of Grub Street is a little startling in its lack of discrimination. We must conclude, then, that as Swift uses the term Grub Street it is pejorative rather than descriptive. This pejorative connotation would explain, for example, why Dryden is made the prototype of the Grub Street hack, rather than Tom Brown who is conspicuously absent from *A Tale of a Tub*.

For Swift, Grub Street, then, was a convenient habitat to which to relegate those Modern writers of whom he did not approve; those who were predominantly Modern in the Ancients-Moderns controversy; those writers he considered turncoats, the dealers in "Factions" and "Apostacies."[5] Grub Street, furthermore, abounded in intramural squabbles, and Swift always found usable grist in the internecine strife within

---

Street (i.e. the Drydens and Bentleys), adept at digressions too, if less overtly than Burton.

[3] See: John Dryden, "Discourse Concerning the Original and Progress of Satire (1693)," *Essays of John Dryden*, ed., W. P. Ker, Oxford, 1926, II, 15-114.

The "Discourse" is an excellent case in point.

[4] See Chap. 4, *supra*.

[5] *A Tale of a Tub*, p. 7 (Apology).

For an excellent analysis of Dryden's various positions, see: Louis I. Bredvold, *Intellectual Milieu of John Dryden*, Ann Arbor, Michigan, 1934.

the ranks of the enemy.[6] That Swift, engaged in one of these squabbles, the Phalaris Controversy (since he considered Bentley and Wotton hacks), and close to the fringes of the controversy over Mr. Bayes (in his satire of Dryden), himself became a member of his own Grub Street is beside the point. It is important to note, however, that Swift's satire on Grub Street is primarily a satire on the criticism rather than the belles-lettres of Grub Street; for if Dryden be considered a hack, Grub Street produced belles-lettres. Swift does not attack Dryden the playwright, nor even Dryden the poet, so much as he attacks Dryden the critic, the translator, the apologist for his changing affiliations in religion and politics. Such satire as Swift levels against Grub Street letters, against D'Urfey the poet of "universal Genius," is incidental and unimportant. It is the learning of the Moderns that Swift satirizes, not their genius; it is the form that this learning assumed in Modern writings that Swift parodies in his structure of *A Tale of a Tub.*

Let us then examine the structure of *A Tale of a Tub* in detail, in order to determine both the intentions and the justness of the parody; towards this purpose the chart accompanying this chapter in included.[7]

I

THE PREFATORY APPARATUS

"Treatises wrote by the same Author...."

Immediately after the title page to *A Tale of a Tub,*[8] we find a list of the "Treatises wrote by the same Author, most

---

[6] See Chap. 2, Sects. I and II, *supra.*

[7] For the idea of this chart I am indebted to Professor James Clifford of Columbia University.

[8] The title page applies to *A Tale of a Tub, Battle of the Books,* and *Mechanical Operation of the Spirit,* in almost all early editions; "Treatises wrote. . ." applies chiefly to the *Tale;* note that in some few early editions the "Treatises wrote. . ." precedes the title page.

of them mentioned in the following Discourses; which will be speedily published." Most of these eleven "Treatises" (eight mentioned in the body of *A Tale of a Tub*, and a ninth furnishing the theme for *The Mechanical Operation of the Spirit*),[9] were never, without doubt, seriously intended for publication, if, indeed, they existed as anything more than titles. But the "Treatises" are more than merely "mentioned" in *A Tale of a Tub*; and the list of these "Treatises" is more than a parody on the self-advertisement of Modern book-sellers and authors. The "Treatises" introduce some of the most important themes of Swift's satire on Modern abuses in religion and learning;[10] they also parody the manner in which Modern learning was expressed. Modern learning, complacent and optimistic, was easily satirized as a learning which expressed itself in general histories, analytical discourses, critical essays; which dissected human nature, operated "Histori-theo-physi-logically,"[11] "*Philosophically, Physically, and*

---

[9] Guthkelch-Smith, *op. cit.*, pp. 345-46.
[10] The "treatises" may be divided into the following:
Religion and Politics
   "*An Analytical Discourse upon Zeal*, Histori-theo-physi-logically *considered.*"
   "*A general History* of Ears."
   "*A modest Defence of the Proceedings of the* Rabble *in all Ages.*"
   "*A Critical Essay upon the Art of* Canting, *Philosophically, Physically, and Musically considered.*"
Science
   "*A Description of the Kingdom of* Absurdities."
   "*A Voyage into* England, *by a Person of Quality in* Terra Australis incognita, *translated from the Original.*"
   "*A Panegyric upon the World.*"
Philosophy
   "*Lectures upon a Dissection of Human Nature.*"
Occult Philosophy
   "*A Panegyrical Essay upon the Number* THREE."
Letters
   "*A Character of the present Set of* Wits *in this Island.*"
   "*A Dissertation upon the principal Productions of* Grub-street."
[11] See the following:
   Robert Boyle, *Some Physico-Theological Considerations about the Possibility of the Resurrection*, London, 1675.
   John Ray, *Three Physico-Theological Discourses*, London, 1713.

Musically"; which was much given to panegyric. The "Treatises," therefore, foreshadow Swift's satirical espousal of Modern learning, and constitute a parody of the attitude with which the Moderns embraced their learning and the terms in which they expressed it.

"An Apology For the, &c."

The "Apology," dated February 1709, and printed for the first time in the fifth (1710) edition of *A Tale of a Tub*, contains Swift's apologia for *A Tale of a Tub*, his defense against the critics of the first three editions of his book, who accused him of immorality, impiety, and plagiarism, and his counter-attack upon those critics as captious, irresponsible, and inept. To the charge that *A Tale of a Tub* was impious, Swift replied in his "Apology" that the author *"will forfeit his Life, if any one Opinion can be fairly deduced from that Book, which is contrary to Religion or Morality."* He protested his orthodoxy, claiming that *A Tale of a Tub* *"Celebrates the Church of* England *as the most perfect of all others in Discipline and Doctrine, it advances no Opinion they reject, nor condemns any they receive."* He apologized, however, for the improprieties in *A Tale of a Tub*, ascribing them to the fact that his manuscript was inaccessible to him at the time of publication, and, therefore, he was unable to correct some of his "youthful Sallies, which from the Grave and Wise may deserve a Rebuke." He therefore announces the date at which his book was written: *"The greatest Part of that Book was finished above thirteen Years since,* 1696, *which was eight Years before it was published."* And to make the purpose of his book clear, he announces his double theme, and his method.

. . . *he thought the numerous and gross Corruptions in Religion and Learning might furnish Matter for a Satyr, that would be useful and diverting: He resolved to proceed in a manner, that should be altogether new, the World having been already too long nauseated with endless Repetitions upon every Subject. The Abuses in Religion he proposed to set forth in the Allegory of the Coats, and the three Brothers, which was to make up the Body of the Discourse. Those in Learning he chose to introduce by way of Digressions. . . .*

It is unfortunate that critics have not availed themselves more fully of the facts provided in the "Apology." The "Apology" supplies the date of *A Tale of a Tub*, it justifies the *Tale's* unique structure, it indicates the double thread of the satire, it relates the *Tale* closely to the Phalaris Controversy, and it emphasizes Swift's moralistic and reforming intentions in writing *A Tale of a Tub*. The "Apology" is scarcely satiric in either tone or intention. It is the norm in *A Tale of a Tub;* to read it as if it were satire is to reject the very real help it offers in our understanding of *A Tale of a Tub*. Nevertheless, it is to be noted that by its very existence alongside of the five other prefatory items the "Apology" helps considerably to reinforce the satirical weight of the whole block of the prefatory apparatus.

"To the Right Honourable, John Lord Sommers."

This dedication, probably written shortly before the publication of *A Tale of a Tub* and certainly after "The Epistle Dedicatory, To His Royal Highness Prince Posterity," is simultaneously a serious dedication to Lord Somers, and a dedication in satire of dedications.[12] To achieve this two-fold

[12] In 1718 appeared an anonymous pamphlet, *Dedication to a Great Man Concerning Dedications,* now attributed to Thomas Gordon of Kircudbright, the Whig journalist. In 1719 appeared an answer to this pamphlet, *Letter to the Reverend Mr. Swift occasioned by a satire said to be written by him Entitled A Dedication to a Great Man concerning dedications.* . . . This answer has been attributed to John Arbuthnot, though with little reason. (See: Lester M. Beattie, *John Arbuthnot, Mathematician and Satirist,* Cambridge, 1935, p. 310.)

It is very interesting, however, that Swift should have been taken for the author of the *Dedication to a Great Man*. And, indeed, in many ways it does recall the dedication to Somers in the *Tale,* and even other parts of

purpose, Swift assumes the character of the ignorant bookseller, on a desperate hunt for the stale, stolen, insincere flat-
teries that constitute a Modern dedication. Thus he flatters
Somers for his military prowess "in mounting a Breach, or
scaling a Wall," for his pedigree, for his "Profound Knowledge in *Algebra, Metaphysicks,* and the Oriental Tongues,"
compliments with which dedicators deal whether they apply
to their patrons or not. But Swift in his own person, as author
of *A Tale of a Tub,* remains in the background and gives
his dignified direction, that his book be given *"to the Worthi-
est," "DETUR DIGNISSIMO,"* "to the sublimest Genius
of the Age, for Wit, Learning, Judgement, Eloquence and
Wisdom." Through this adroit raillery, an apparent reflection
upon someone which turns out to be a real compliment,
(Somers as he was only flattered by the bookseller and as he
was eventually truly praised by the author) Swift achieved
simultaneously a handsome dedication and a satire on dedications.

The extent to which the dedication to Somers contains
parody of the mercenary and fulsome dedications of the
Moderns may be determined by reading almost any contemporary dedication. Let us, however, examine a dedication
of Dryden's, since in the "Digression in the Modern Kind"
Swift accused Dryden of having exhausted the possibilities
of dedications. The "Discourse concerning the Original and
Progress of Satire," simultaneously dedication and preface

---

that book. The author of the *Dedication* satirizes the mercenary character
of dedications, draws an itemized bill upon his patron, and evaluates in
pounds, shillings, and pence the price of each piece of flattery: learning,
eloquence, justice, honor, courage, wit, humor, etc., etc., all in a manner
quite reminiscent of Swift's dedication to Somers.

Undoubtedly Swift did not write the *Dedication;* it is, however, of
interest to us as a kind of plagiarism of the *Tale.* The *Dedication* satirizes
dedications in very much the same terms, though with considerably less
skill, as the dedication to Somers. And, in a way, the *Dedication* serves as
justification of Swift's satire on dedications in *A Tale of a Tub.*

to Dryden's translations from Juvenal and Persius, is an excellent case in point. This dedication and preface equals the translations in bulk and certainly outweighs them in importance. It embodies many aspects of Dryden's manner which so irritated Swift. But more significant is the extraordinary impact of the fulsomeness of the "Discourse" once the reader relegates to the background his very real admiration of the "Discourse" as literary criticism, and his tacit acceptance of superlatives as a necessary concomitant to patronage. Even granted the fact that Dryden sincerely admired Dorset's work, the extravagance of his dedication is eminently susceptible to parody.

Dryden tells Dorset that he is universally beloved; "Titus Vespasian was not more the delight of human-kind." Dorset is at the "meridian"; "the daylight [is] at high noon; and all who have the benefit of sight, can look up as well, and see the sun." Dryden has long known Dorset "as the restorer of poetry, the greatest genius, the truest judge, and the best patron." Dorset enjoys right reason, good sense, good nature, beneficence, candor, and possesses those "heights . . . from a happy, abundant, and native genius: which are as inborn" to him "as they were to Shakespeare; and for aught I know to Homer"; Dorset excels all other English writers "in all the several parts of poetry" which he has "undertaken to adorn. The most vain, and the most ambitious of our age . . . have yielded the first place without dispute; and have been arrogantly content to be esteemed as second. . . ." His lyric poems are the "delight and wonder of this age, and will be the envy of the next." As for his satire:

There is more of salt in all your verses, than I have seen in any of the Moderns, or even of the Ancients; but you have been sparing of the gall, by which means you have pleased all readers, and offended none. Donne alone, of all our countrymen, had your talent; but was not happy enough to arrive at your versification;

and were he translated into numbers, and English, he would yet be wanting in the dignity of expression.

Only in heroic poetry, in their Homer and Virgil, were the Ancients unique.

. . . in Tragedy and Satire, I offer myself to maintain against some of our Modern critics, that this age and the last, particularly in England, have excelled the Ancients in both those kinds; and I would instance in Shakespeare of the former, in your Lordship in the latter sort.

If Dorset has any imperfection it lies in the fact that like Virgil he has not written enough.[13]

It is not suggested that the "Discourse" is the specific source of the parody in Swift's dedication to Somers. It is, however, abundantly clear that after reading many such contemporary dedications, Swift had materials and justification enough for his parody on dedications in the dedication to "The Right Honourable, John Lord Sommers."

"The Bookseller to the Reader"

"The Bookseller to the Reader" (1704), undoubtedly written by Swift, has principally served, since the addition of the "Apology" of 1710, to swell the bulk of the prefatory apparatus in *A Tale of a Tub*. It contains nothing factual that is not provided more fully by the "Apology"; like the "Apology" it reveals the date of the composition of *A Tale of a Tub*, the fact that Swift did not have his manuscript about him at publication, and it insists upon the anonymity of the author. It is written in that tone of mock humility and tentativeness through which Swift managed so successfully, in many parts of *A Tale of a Tub*, to achieve the effect of the most arrogant certainty and assurance. The bookseller announces that he postponed printing *A Tale of a Tub* because

[13] Dryden, "Discourse Concerning the Original and Progress of Satire," in *Essays of John Dryden*, pp. 15-26, *passim*.

he had "better work" on hand; he fears, however, a Modern, Grub Street refinement[14] upon a stolen copy of the *Tale*, and hence he decides to publish. He is frankly puzzled by the meaning of the work he is publishing:

If any Gentleman will please to furnish me with a Key, in order to explain the more difficult Parts, I shall very gratefully acknowledge the Favour and print it by it self.

Swift tells us later, in the "Further Digression" (Section x), of his gratification that "Fate has flung me into so blessed an Age for the mutual Felicity of *Booksellers* and *Authors*, whom I may safely affirm to be at this Day the only satisfied Parties in *England*." The "Bookseller to the Reader" is, therefore, an example in passing of one of these Modern, "wonderful Civilities" among authors, booksellers, and readers.

"The Epistle Dedicatory, To His Royal Highness Prince Posterity"

Unlike the bookseller's dedication to Lord Somers, the author's dedication to Prince Posterity, written considerably earlier than the dedication to Somers, is not a satire on dedications. It does, however, provide another "god-father" for *A Tale of a Tub* in parody of the multiple dedications of the Moderns, and it recalls Swift's satire on the "Multiplicity of *God-fathers*" to Dryden's *Virgil* in his "Introduction" to *A Tale of a Tub*. The "Epistle" to Prince Posterity is principally a mock panegyric on Modern writers, who kept a weather eye on Posterity, "the sole Arbiter of the Productions of human Wit, in this polite and most accomplish'd Age." The number of such Modern "appellants" to Prince Posterity, Swift insists, was very large.

[14] Cervantes, Boccalini, La Bruyère, Quevedo, and Boccaccio were all "refined" and fitted to the "Humour of the Age." (See: *A Tale of a Tub*, p. 29 [Bookseller to the Reader], and n. 1 by the editors.)

Swift expostulates with Posterity against his *"Governour,"* Time. As a mock-Modern, and no friend to Time as the Ancients are, Swift, "well-informed of his [Time's] Designs," knows that in the future when Posterity is grown out of his nonage, Time will try to persuade him that "our Age is almost wholly illiterate, and has hardly produc'd one Writer upon any Subject." And when Posterity will ask for a Modern work, Time will "pretend it a Demonstration that there never were any, because they are not to be found." Therefore Swift informs Posterity that, even as he writes, Time is exterminating Modern works in many ways, that he is maliciously destroying the infants "before they have so much as learnt their *Mother-Tongue* to beg for pity." To protest Time's lie that the "Age is altogether Unlearned," Swift attempts to adduce proof of the Moderns' right to Posterity's regard by a "copious List of *Titles*"; but a few hours after the "Originals" came out, "The *Memorial of them was lost among Men, their Place was no more to be found.*" Swift, therefore, must cite for Posterity his "cotemporary [sic] brethren," the very latest Moderns: Dryden, Tate, Durfey, Rymer, Dennis, Bentley, and Wotton. In emulation of his fellow Moderns, Swift presents Posterity with "a faithful Abstract drawn from the Universal Body of all Arts and Sciences"; and he promises Posterity a "character of the present Set of *Wits* in our Nation: Their Persons I shall describe particularly, and at Length, their Genius and Understandings in Mignature."

A mock panegyric on Modern writers, the "Epistle Dedicatory, to his Royal Highness Prince Posterity," achieves its point through Swift's implicit satire on the idea of Progress. The Moderns, believing that they had progressed beyond the Ancients in many ways, were, indeed, confident of their place in posterity. That their confidence was misguided Swift satirically ascribes not to their own worthlessness but to the malicious machinations of Time. We must remember, in addition, that the idea of Progress also hypothesized a continual progress in the future. And given this faith in indefinite progress, every Modern was liable to displacement in Posterity's regard by a later Modern. Hence the double edge of Swift's satire in the "Epistle" to Prince Posterity: the everlasting Moderns, who die in their infancy, appealing to a posterity whom they themselves have determined to displace them by greater, because more lately born, infants. Swift's choice of the allegorical method in the "Epistle" to satirize the Moderns' faith in progress was particularly happy, for the child Posterity, the prince in his nonage under the domination of his governor Time, recalls the whole history of the Ancients-Moderns controversy in England, the dwarf-giant image and the *juventus mundi, aetatis saeculi* theme, about which so much of the controversy centered.

But Swift's satire in the "Epistle" to Prince Posterity has more than two edges. Even though allegory (and the "Epistle" is the only section of Swift's satire on learning that is developed allegorically) cannot in its over-all structure parody anything except another allegory, it does allow room for internal parody, parody in details. Note, then, the first few lines of the "Epistle":

I here present *Your Highness* with the Fruits of a very few leisure Hours, stollen from the short Intervals of a World of Business, and of an Employment quite alien from such Amusements as this:

as they recall Sir Richard Blackmore's preface to *Prince Arthur*:

If I have not succeeded [in *Prince Arthur*], my disappointment will be the less, in that Poetry has been so far from being my Business and Profession, that it has imploy'd but a small part of my Time; and then, but as my Recreation, and the Entertainment of my idle hours.[15]

[15] Sir Richard Blackmore, *Prince Arthur*, London, 1696. (See: Guthkelch-Smith, *op. cit.*, p. 182, n. 2.)

This modest depreciation of a writer's work, disingenuous because the depreciation was as often as not coupled with a plea for posterity's regard, echoes through the scientific writings of the late seventeenth century. Even the *Philosophical Transactions* of the Royal Society are punctuated with apologies like this: "In these Rude Collections, which are onely the Gleanings of my private diversions in Broken Hours. . . ."[16] And Robert Boyle frequently justified his scientific and religious writings by explaining that they were the diversions of his idle hours.[17] For the gentleman, in abandoning his dilettante business for utilitarian business, felt moved to apologize for his utilitarianism lest he be confused with the plebeian. And, no doubt, the plebeian felt moved to emulate the gentleman by pretending that he too had more important business somewhere in the background.

Thus the "Epistle" to Prince Posterity is satiric of the Moderns' faith in progress and of those who, disingenuously or not, expected to live forever upon the diversions of their idle hours; and the "Epistle" is also a parody on style. It is a parody on the style which we now call the "baroque" or the "anti-Ciceronian";[18] a style which in the hands of Sir Thomas Browne and John Milton achieved a complex imaginative power; a style which in the hands of less able writers became merely a heavy, digressive, asyntactical morass. The aspect of the baroque style which Swift parodies chiefly in the Epistle is the loose structure of the sentence, composed

---

Swift read *Prince Arthur* in 1696/7-1697/8. (Sheridan, *op. cit.*, p. 22.)

Swift probably enjoyed the fact that Blackmore was attacked by Dryden and Dennis. (See: "Blackmore, Sir Richard," *DNB*.)

[16] Henry Oldenburg, "To the Royal Society," prefacing the first volume of the collected *Philosophical Transactions*, 1665/6.

[17] See: Robert Boyle, *Occasional Reflections Upon Several Subjects*, London, 1665, "Introductory Preface."

[18] Morris W. Croll, "Baroque Style in Prose," in *Studies in English Philology in Honor of Frederick Klaeber*, eds., Kemp Malone and Martin B. Ruud, Minneapolis, 1929, pp. 427-56.

of many separate and digressive members only loosely tied together. Note the five separate members of the opening sentence of the "Epistle," its sententious weight, as Swift, the mock Modern, makes his disingenuous plea to Posterity's regard:

Sir,

I Here present *Your Highness* with the Fruits of a very few leisure Hours, stollen from the short Intervals of a World of Business, and of an Employment quite alien from such Amusements as this: The poor Production of that Refuse of Time which has lain heavy upon my Hands, during a long Prorogation of Parliament, a great Dearth of Forein News, and a tedious Fit of rainy Weather: For which, and other Reasons, it cannot chuse extreamly to deserve such a Patronage as that of *Your Highness,* whose numberless Virtues in so few Years, make the World look upon You as the future Example to all Princes: For altho' *Your Highness* is hardly got clear of Infancy, yet has the universal learned World already resolv'd upon appealing to Your Future Dictates with the lowest and most resigned Submission: Fate having decreed You sole Arbiter of the Productions of human Wit, in this polite and most accomplish'd Age.

Here we see Swift's talent for parody at its best, in the perfect union of matter and method.

"The Preface"

Swift's "Preface" to *A Tale of a Tub,* the last item in the prefatory apparatus, is the most important of the prefatory sections and, indeed, one of the most important sections in the whole book, as if Swift, satirical of Modern formlessness, decided to relegate some of his most significant ideas to a preface, where they do not belong. "The Preface" is simultaneously an exposition of some of these ideas and a satire, and in part a parody, on Modern prefaces.

In its latter function the "Preface" is reinforced and clarified by the "Digression in the Modern Kind," part of which,

Swift tells us, is, in effect, another preface; but afraid of sati-
ating the reader at the outset and in order to swell his volume,
he couched his second preface in a digression. This confusion,
obviously, is exactly the effect Swift intended to create. In
the "Digression in the Modern Kind," Swift informs us
that "the establish'd Custom of our newest Authors" is to
insist upon their own "Excellencies and other Mens De-
faults."[19] This custom Swift honors in his "Preface" to *A
Tale of a Tub* as he proceeds to parody Dryden. In parody
of Dryden's ingenuous faith in the reader's continuing interest
through tedious relations of his private mishaps and cogita-
tions, Swift informs his readers that he composed his book in
a garret bed, that he endured a long course of Physick, and
that he sharpened his "Invention with Hunger," all like a
true Grub Street brother. On the one occasion in the "Preface"
when Swift is moved to depart from his own virtues, in a
sudden access of humility he engages in a kind of parodic
debate with Dryden. Dryden had explained that:

. . . wit in the Poet . . . is no other than the faculty of imagination
in the writer, which, like a nimble spaniel, beats over and ranges
through the field of memory, till it springs the quarry it hunted
after; . . . So then, the first happiness of the poet's imagination is
properly invention, or finding of the thought. . . . the quickness
of the imagination is seen in the invention. . . .[20]

To which Swift replied:

Thrice have I forced my Imagination to make the *Tour* of my
Invention, and thrice has it returned empty; the latter having
been wholly drained by the following Treatise. Not so, my more
successful Brethren the *Moderns*, who will by no means let slip
a Preface or Dedication, without some notable distinguishing
Stroke, to surprize the Reader at the Entry, and kindle a Wonderful Expectation of what is to ensue.

In the other half of his duty as a Modern, to expatiate on

[19] *A Tale of a Tub*, p. 132 (Digression in the Modern Kind).
[20] Dryden, "Preface of Annus Mirabilis (1667)," in *Essays of John Dryden*, I, 14, 15.

other writers' faults, "declaiming, according to the Custom, against the Multitude of Writers whereof the whole Multitude of Writers most reasonably complains," Swift is not so successful. He sets down a few stock complaints, garnered, as he says, from a few hundred prefaces:

For a Man to set up for a Writer, when the Press swarms with, &c.
Another;

The Tax upon Paper does not lessen the Number of Scribblers, who daily pester, &c.

But Swift need not have read many prefaces for this piece of parody. A passage in Dryden's "Discourse concerning the Original and Progress of Satire" recalls not only the reasonable complaints but indicates the biographical tediousness, mentioned above, to which Dryden was given in his prefaces.

And indeed, a provocation is almost necessary, in behalf of the world, that you might be induced sometimes to write: and in relation to a multitude of scribblers, who daily pester the world with their insufferable stuff, that they might be discouraged from writing any more. I complain not of their lampoons and libels, though I have been a public mark for many years. . . . And for my morals, if they are not proof against their attacks, let me be thought by posterity, what those authors would be thought, if any memory of them, or of their writings, could endure so long as to another age.[21]

Apparently Swift endured not only "a long Course of Physick, and a great want of Money," as he wrote *A Tale of a Tub,* but a long course of Dryden too. The whole big bubble of Swift's parody on Dryden, however, bursts suddenly, to magnificent effect, when Swift, stepping out of his Modern character for a moment, tells the parable of the fat mountebank in Leicester Fields, who kept complaining about the crowd until the weaver inelegantly stopped him: "*Is not the*

[21] Dryden, "Discourse Concerning the Original and Progress of Satire," in *Essays of John Dryden,* II, 21, 22.

*Place as free for us as for you? Bring your own Guts to a
reasonable Compass (and be d -- n'd) and then I'll engage
we shall have room enough for us all."*

"The Preface," however, as we have said, is more than a
satire on prefaces; it also contains Swift's earnest evaluation
of his medium, the theory and practice of satire, and it contains
Swift's most effective satire on Modern wit.

Swift begins his "Preface" by explaining the title and the
purpose of *A Tale of a Tub* as a kind of project to prevent
the Wits from "tossing and sporting with the *Commonwealth*," reminiscent, incidentally, of Sprat's championship
of the new science as a promoter of peace in Britain.[22] In
his satirical espousal of Modernity Swift proceeds to spend
a large portion of the "Preface" eulogizing Modern wit and
wits. Swift scarcely defines wit, and yet, as he uses the term,
satirically or otherwise, throughout *A Tale of a Tub,* his
meaning is very clear. In his use of the word wit Swift satirizes
not only some several Moderns, but all the Moderns; they
lack wit even as they lack taste. Whatsoever was false, dis-
honest, stupid, dull, pretentious; whatsoever was crackbrained,
parasitical, obscure, evanescent, perverse, carping, canting:[23]
that was the wit of the Moderns, those who were witty because they could be neither "wise nor sound," the very Moderns, their "Taste of Wit, calculated for the present Month
of *August,* 1697."[24] On the other hand, that faculty and product of the efficient intellect, "that noblest Gift of humane
nature," that quality which either accompanies or is the result
of learning, judgment, eloquence, wisdom, taste, and candor,
that "most agreeable gift of mankind," that was true wit
and operated as agent and guard for the serious and social
responsibility of art.[25] And the Moderns in *A Tale of a Tub*

[22] See: Sprat, *op. cit.,* pp. 437-38.
[23] See: *A Tale of a Tub,* pp. 23, 25, 39, 41, 42, 45.
[24] *Ibid.,* p. 44 (Preface).
[25] *Ibid.,* p. 18 (Apology); p. 23 (Dedication to Somers).

have it not, neither in criticism, letters, philosophy, nor in science.

The last several pages of "The Preface" are devoted to Swift's mock panegyric on Modern satire. Beginning with: " 'Tis a great Ease to my Conscience that I have writ so elaborate and useful a Discourse without one grain of Satyr intermixt. . . ." Swift disclaims against the "satyrical itch" of his contemporaries, that itch which Sir William Temple had found detrimental to piety, virtue, and learning,[26] and which Swift himself had, in *The Battle of the Books*, related to the poison of the spider, prototype of the Moderns, *"feeding upon the* Insects *and* Vermin *of the Age."*[27] Contemporary satirists, Swift tells us in the "Preface," whipped their public that they might the more profitably flay; and the public stands, like a docile schoolboy, with its breeches down, "ready Hors'd for Discipline." Contemporary satirists, he proceeds, are inept and toothless, though foul-breathed, and they wield a rusty razor.

Then, having explained the two general defects of contemporary satire, Swift continues his indictment in a particularly effective way, using satire both as his technique and matter. He writes a mock panegyric on contemporary satire, and a satire on contemporary panegyric. In his little panegyric on his brother satirists, he tells us that the public prefers satire and that it praises satirists in proportion to the lashes they deliver. Satire, which has a wealth of themes in vice and folly, is neither an exhaustible subject nor dull, unlike panegyric which deals in virtue, a slender and limited subject. And even were satire not the fruitful field it is, it is safer than panegyric, which causes envy. All the panegyrist need do is to memorize a series of laudatory terms, and ring changes upon them. The changes, the terms, like the ideas, are few.

---

[26] Temple, *Essay*, p. 486.
[27] *The Battle of the Books*, p. 234.

And fortunately so, for panegyric, being specific and pointed, breeds envy; whereas satire is general and hurts no one.

The last point, the general nature of contemporary satire, leads to Swift's contrast between contemporary satire and Attic satire, the most significant section of Swift's discussion.

In the *Attick* Commonwealth, it was the Privilege and Birthright of every Citizen and Poet, to rail aloud and in publick, or to expose upon the Stage by Name, any Person they pleased, tho' of the greatest Figure, whether a *Creon* [*sic*] an *Hyperbolus,* an *Alcibiades,* or a *Demosthenes*: But on the other side, the least reflecting word let fall against the *People* in general, was immediately caught up, and revenged upon the Authors, however considerable for their Quality or their Merits. Whereas in *England* it is just the Reverse of all this. Here, you may securely display your utmost *Rhetorick* against Mankind, in the Face of the World; . . . And when you have done, the whole Audience, far from being offended, shall return you thanks as a Deliverer of precious and useful Truths. . . . 'Tis but a *Ball* bandied to and fro, and every Man carries a *Racket* to strike it from himself among the rest of the Company.

Swift's reference to Cleon, Hyperbolus, and Alcibiades connects his statement indisputably with Aristophanes. For the rest, Swift refers to the pseudo-Xenephon *On the Polity of the Athenians* written in the same year as Aristophanes' *Knights.* Cleon, the demagogue who stole the victory at Pylos, is satirized in the *Knights;* and his exploitation of Demos, the populace, is satirized in *Wasps.*[28] Hyperbolus, second in demagoguery only to Cleon, appears in *Knights.* And Alcibiades, as the rich young man about town, is the Pheidippides of *Clouds.*[29]

Several instructive parallels may be drawn between Aristophanes and Swift. In the wars between ancients and mod-

---

[28] Gilbert Murray, *Aristophanes,* New York, 1933, Chaps. II, III.

Aristophanes, *Plays,* ed. and trans., Benjamin Bickley Rogers, London, 1924, 3 vols. (Vol. I, *Acharnians, Clouds, Knights, Wasps;* Vol. II, *Peace, Birds, Frogs;* Vol. III, *Lysistrata, Thesmophoriazusae, Ecclesiazusae, Plutus.*)

[29] R. C. Jebb, "Aristophanes," *Encyclopedia Britannica* (14th ed.).

erns in their respective times, Aristophanes and Swift were unalterably opposed to the modern, the worlds they never made. Like Swift, Aristophanes lived in a period of changing ideals and standards. In his time a new scepticism towards religion was developing, materialism and atomism had been propounded, art was growing less austere and more refined, and popular demagoguery was replacing the limited democracy. The spirit of reform was abroad; radicalism, unconventionality, relaxed morals, and free thought flourished. Men of essentially conservative, aristocratic, and moralistic temper, both Aristophanes and Swift were dedicated to satirizing the new in order to buttress the old. Both joined their high moral purpose to their great satiric gifts for the achievement of social reform. Both were passionate, witty, censorious men, and each had a kind of licentious virtuosity which frequently obscured his high moral purpose. And both fought a losing battle.[30] Indeed, many of the themes in Aristophanes sound very familiar to the student of *A Tale of a Tub*: the satire on the new education, new philosophy, and new religion in *Clouds;* the new popular demagoguery in *Knights;* and the new rationalism and materialism in *Birds.* Even the form of the Aristophanic comedy, the elaborate parody, symmetry, and debate between two opposing principles, recalls the ingenious symmetry of *A Tale of a Tub.*

But what most clearly connects Swift's discussion of satire in the "Preface" to *A Tale of a Tub* with Aristophanes, more than Swift's contrast between Attic and English satire, more than his enumeration of Cleon, Hyperbolus, and Alcibiades, and even more than the obvious parallels between Swift and Aristophanes in their respective eras, is Swift's insistence upon personal, *ad hominem* satire, "private taxing";

[30] See the following:
Louis E. Lord, *Aristophanes*, New York, 1927, *passim.*
Philip Whaley Harsh, *Handbook of Classical Drama*, Stanford University, California, 1944, pp. 264-312.

for in this insistence he goes counter to the whole stream of Renaissance theory and practice of satire.[31] One of the distinguishing characteristics of the Aristophanic comedy is the use of personal invective; the attack was always extremely personalized. The fact that Aristophanes frequently generalized his satiric characters does not make his satire any less personal and pointed. Thus, though Cleon is mentioned by name only once in *Knights,* there is not the slightest doubt that the Paphlagonian is clearly meant to stand for the demagogue Cleon more than for the type of the demagogue. (Aristotle, in differentiating between vices and follies, exempted Aristophanic comedy from the stream of legitimate satire as lampoon.) The Middle Comedy then tended to substitute the innuendo or suggestion and exaggeration for personal abuse, a tendency which the New Comedy strengthened. Renaissance theory and practice of satire, developing in this stream, was always opposed to the personal attack. Even Jonson, who merged Aristophanic comedy with the spirit of formal verse satire in the evolution of his "comicall satyres," disapproved of Aristophanes' portrait of Socrates as invective. It is to be noted, then, that Swift went directly against the spirit of Renaissance satire in approving, as he does both theoretically and in actual practice in *A Tale of a Tub,* "*ad hominem*" satire like that of Aristophanes, and in depreciating the value of innuendo, suggestion, exaggeration, and satire of types rather than of individuals. The only way the Renaissance could find to justify the harshness and license of Aristophanic comedy was to consider it an outgrowth of the old satyrs. Thus Renaissance satirists insisted that they were impersonal so that the guiltless need not take offense; and inasmuch as many were guilty, they said, satire was un-

[31] For the survey of the history of satire in this paragraph, see: Oscar James Campbell, *Comicall Satyre and Shakespeare's Troilus and Cressida,* San Marino, California, 1938.

popular. And it was exactly because satire was so general that Swift found contemporary satire futile. No one was offended; everyone enjoyed it because he thought he was guiltless; and because everyone enjoyed it, Swift found that contemporary satire failed of its moral purpose, reform. Only the vague populace (Demos, whom Aristophanes never excoriated) was attacked in contemporary satire. Swift's aim was topical, not typical; it is for this reason that he suggested that it was time to get back to an older, a personal and invective kind of satire. Whether he knew it or not, he had already done so in *A Tale of a Tub*.

It is by no means suggested that in *A Tale of a Tub* Swift sat down deliberately to write a prose narrative satire in imitation of Aristophanic comedy. Indeed, long before Swift's time Aristophanic comedy had ceased to be a literary kind; and Swift disapproved of Aristophanes as profane and licentious. But it is childish to suppose that Swift wrote his satire as ingenuously as any Grub Street hack airing his personal antipathies. He was writing to reform and delight. It is the Grub Street hacks he accuses of the "satyrical itch." And it is significant that when Swift abandoned his original literary kinds, the Pindaric ode and the verse satire, he turned, in *The Battle of the Books,* to another, an equally approved kind, the mock heroic epic. In *A Tale of a Tub,* though in form remote from the classics, Swift achieved a spirit of satire more anciently classical than the spirit of Horace, Juvenal, and Persius, the spirit of Aristophanes. The vague comparisons between Swift and Juvenal, Lucian, and Erasmus are commonplace. It is here suggested that what links Swift with each of these satirists (at least so far as *A Tale of a Tub* is concerned) is essentially the spirit of Aristophanes. What is Juvenalian, Lucianic, and Erasmian in Swift is contained in their common heritage of Aristophanes.

The Satiric Intention of the Prefatory Apparatus

Each of the six prefatory sections, as we have tried to show, individually constitutes an effective satire on, and in some details a parody of, individual phases of the pride, pretentiousness, and ignorance of Modern writers. Together, as a prefatory block, these six sections, along with the marginal notes and the footnotes,[32] constitute an elaborate parody on Modern writing, and hence on Modern learning, a thing of dedications, prefaces, self-advertisement, apologies, and explanations, sterile and formless. To see the justice and propriety of Swift's parody one need but glance at the table of contents of John Dryden's *The Works of Virgil, containing his Pastorals, Georgics and Aeneis.* Translated into English Verse. London, Printed for Jacob Tonson, 1697.[33]

[32] Though not strictly part of the prefatory apparatus, the footnotes and marginal notes in *A Tale of a Tub* add to the paraphernalia surrounding the tale proper, and in themselves they contain a good deal of satire.

The marginal notes (along with which the comments on the hiatuses in the text, like *"hic multa desiderantur,"* must be considered), were undoubtedly written by Swift, though some pretend to be written by someone other than the author. "Some of them are nothing less than an integral part of the text, the humour being transferred to the margin from the body of the page." (Guthkelch-Smith, *op. cit.*, pp. xx-xxiii.) They appeared in the first and in all subsequent editions of the *Tale.*

The footnotes, first printed in the fifth edition of the *Tale,* are by Swift, some of them, however, being signed quotations from Wotton's "Observations upon the Tale of a Tub" appended to the third (1705) edition of his *Reflections.* Thus Wotton, one of the *Tale's* chief critics, is made an accessory to the book.

Together, all these notes constitute a parody on the elaborate annotations of contemporary writers, at the same time that they serve a useful purpose in providing Swift more elbow room for satire. They serve a variety of purposes, a straightforward indication of his sources, explanation, mock rebukes to himself in the character of another person, correction, disagreement, amplification, etc. The notes are satirical, as no reader of seventeenth century works can fail to see, of a current style in writing.

[33] Hugh Macdonald, *John Dryden, A Bibliography of Early Editions and of Drydeniana,* Oxford, 1939, pp. 56, 57.

Note that in addition to all these god-fathers apparent from the table of contents, Dryden adds several in his "Postscript." (See: Davis, *Satire of Jonathan Swift,* p. 31.)

Title Page
Dedication to Hugh, Lord Clifford
The Life of Pub. Virgilius Maro
Preface to the Pastorals
Commendatory Verses to Dryden
Errata and Direction to Binders
Names of Subscribers to the Cuts of Virgil,
    each Subscription being Five Guineas
Names of the Second Subscribers
Text of the Pastorals
Dedication to Philip, Earl of Chesterfield
An Essay on the Georgics
Text of the Georgics
Dedication to John, Lord Marquess of Normanby
Text of the Aeneid
Postscript to the Reader
Notes and Observations on Virgil's Works in English

Furthermore, inasmuch as the prefatory apparatus is satire and parody on Modern writing, it is to be considered as satire on learning along with the digressions. Against the five sections of religious allegory in *A Tale of a Tub* (Sections II, IV, VI, VIII, XI) we must balance not only the five digressions (Sections III, V, IX, X) as well as most of the "Introduction" and "Conclusion," but also the six prefatory items. In addition, within the allegorical sections religious abuses are often satirized by being related to abuses in learning: Catholicism is discredited by being related to science, Nonconformity by occultism. *A Tale of a Tub*, then, may well have been conceived as principally a religious allegory, a satire on the abuses in religion, but it emerged as principally a satire on abuses in Modern learning. Whether Swift was aware of this or not is debatable.[34] Nevertheless, there is a certain appropriate

[34] It is true that in the "Apology" to the *Tale*, Swift seems to imply that "the greatest part" of his book is the religious allegory. "Greatest" it may have loomed at the time in importance, especially in the light of the criticism the allegory provoked. But, given a historical perspective, the satire on the abuses in learning is scarcely subsidiary in either bulk or importance, though as the work of a clergyman, it could not have evoked

irony in the fact that Swift developed what we believe to be his main theme, the abuses in learning, in introductions, prefaces, dedications, digressions, and conclusions; his tale proper, the religious allegory, is, after all, only subsidiary, like many another Modern tale. Indeed, if our interpretation of *A Tale of a Tub* be correct, there is an appropriate irony in the critical history of the *Tale*: that which Swift labeled preface, introduction, digression, etc., for the purpose of parody, criticism has largely been overlooked as being prefatory, introductory, and digressive in real earnest; whereas the tale proper, actually only a digression, has been accorded all proper attention.

II

THE SYMMETRY OF ALLEGORY AND DIGRESSION

Section I,

"The Introduction"

"The Introduction" is the bridge between the prefatory apparatus and the beginning of Swift's tale in Section II. With philosophical thoroughness, Swift establishes his platform through his "Physico-logical Scheme of Oratorial Receptacles or Machines," from which, since philosophers' *"Edifices in the Air"* are "often out of *Sight,* and ever out of *Hearing,"* he can be "heard in a Crowd." These oratorial machines are: "the *Pulpit,* the *Ladder,* and the *Stage-Itinerant.*"

---

so much controversy as the allegory. Besides, for the general public, the Ancients-Moderns controversy was by this time an old, beaten story, however militant the chief combatants in the latest skirmish may have been.

By the *Pulpit* are adumbrated the Writings of our *Modern Saints* in *Great Britain,* as they have spiritualized and refined them from the Dross and Grossness of *Sense* and *Human Reason.* . . . The *Ladder* is an adequate Symbol of *Faction* and *Poetry.* . . . Under the *Stage-Itinerant* are couched those Productions designed for the Pleasure and Delight of Mortal Man; such as *Six-peny-worth* of *Wit,* Westminster *Drolleries, Delightful Tales, Compleat Jesters,* and the like; by which the Writers of and for *GRUB-STREET,* have in these latter Ages so nobly triumph'd over *Time;* have clipt his Wings, pared his Nails, filed his Teeth, turn'd back his Hour-Glass, blunted his Scythe, and drawn the Hob-Nails out of his Shoes. It is under this Classis, I have presumed to list my present Treatise, being just come from having the Honor conferred upon me, to be adopted a Member of that Illustrious Fraternity.

The pulpit and ladder as platforms for the religious and political dissenters respectively are obvious enough in their implications. Swift's choice of the "stage-itinerant" as his own and his fellow Grub-Streeters' platform is puzzling. Certainly Swift did not intend to relate this oratorial machine to the theater, for he neither wrote plays, nor did he mention any plays as being delivered from this platform. The "stage" of the "stage-itinerant" must then be understood to be synonymous with platform, and insofar as the Grub Streeter was serviceable upon any occasion and carried his materials about with him, he may be said to have been "itinerant."[35]

[35] Two sets of eight illustrations each are included in the Guthkelch-Smith edition of the *Tale.* The first set, which appeared for the first time in the fifth edition of the *Tale,* was made under the auspices of Bernard Lens and John Stuart. The second set, not discovered until 1831, in the possession of the Fountaine family, was in some way connected with Sir Andrew Fountaine. The two sets of illustrations are not completely parallel in subject matter. One of the original engravings shows Jack, in a barrel mounted on a pulpit, blowing oracular gusts of wind which visibly affect his oratory. In the corresponding Fountaine cut Jack is similarly mounted, and similarly windy, but his audience is bored and somnolent. To one side of this (Fountaine) illustration there is a panel showing a criminal mounting a ladder, and right next to the ladder, an outdoor stage on which appear two actors. Behind them is a curtain. The illustrator, then, must have considered a "stage-itinerant" an orthodox, theater stage. (See: Guthkelch-

In several of the prefatory items mentioned above Swift writes as a member of Grub Street; but not until the "Introduction" does he become its formal apologist. He defends his society against the encroachments of the "two *Junior* start-up Societies," Gresham's and Will's; and in the face of a "superficial Vein among many Readers of the present Age," he engages upon a "compleat and laborious Dissertation upon the prime Productions of our Society, which besides their beautiful Externals for the Gratification of superficial Readers, have darkly and deeply couched under them, the most finished and refined Systems of all Sciences and Arts." Not only does Swift defend his society, but he assumes the style, on occasion, of one of his most eminent brethren, John Dryden, whom he alternately praises satirically and parodies. Dryden recurs, in one way or another, through much of Swift's "Introduction": as part of his "laborious Dissertation upon the prime Productions" of Grub Street, Swift has annotated:

The *Hind and Panther.* This is the Master-piece of a famous Writer now living, intended for a compleat Abstract of sixteen thousand Schoolmen from *Scotus* to *Bellarmin.*

Dryden is satirized as the canny multiplier of god-fathers to his *Virgil;* and finally, he is the source for a whole paragraph of parody:

These Notices may serve to give the Learned Reader an Idea as well as a Taste of what the whole Work is likely to produce: wherein I have now altogether circumscribed my Thoughts and my Studies; and if I can bring it to a Perfection before I die, shall reckon I have well employ'd the poor Remains of an unfortunate Life. This indeed is more than I can justly expect from a Quill worn to the Pith in the Service of the State, in *Pro's* and *Con's* upon *Popish Plots*, and *Meal Tubs*, . . . From an Understanding and a Conscience, thread-bare and ragged with perpetual turning; From a Head broken in a hundred places, by the Malignants of

Smith, *op. cit.*, pp. xxii-xxvi; the two engravings mentioned are inserted between pp. 56 and 57 of the text.)

the opposite Factions, . . . Four-score and eleven Pamphlets have I written under three Reigns, and for the Service of six and thirty Factions. But finding the State has no farther Occasion for Me and my Ink, I retire willingly to draw it out into Speculations more becoming a Philosopher, having, to my unspeakable Comfort, passed a long Life, with a Conscience void of Offence.

Note, in comparison, the "Postscript to the Reader" to Dryden's *Virgil*:

What Virgil wrote in the vigour of his age, in plenty and at ease, I have undertaken to translate in my declining years; struggling with wants, oppressed with sickness, curbed in my genius, liable to be misconstrued in all I write; and my judges, if they are not very equitable, already prejudiced against me, by the lying character which has been given them of my morals. Yet steady to my principles, and not dispirited with my afflictions, I have, by the blessing of God on my endeavours, overcome all difficulties, and, in some measure, acquitted myself of the debt which I owed the public when I undertook this work. . . . since the Revolution, I have wholly renounced that talent [satire]. For who would give physic to the great, when he is uncalled?—to do his patient no good, and endanger himself for his prescription? Neither am I ignorant, but I may justly be condemned for many of those faults of which I have too liberally arraigned others. . . . Tis enough for me, if the Government will let me pass unquestioned.[36]

Clearly, Swift intended to suggest that Dryden was preeminent not only when mounted upon the stage itinerant but on the pulpit, and that he came close to the ladder too.

Section II *and Section* III, "A Digression Concerning Criticks"

The unity between Section II of *A Tale of a Tub* and Section III, "A Digression Concerning Criticks," is achieved through the symbol of the tailor, the tailor-deity of sartorism, and the tailor-critic of Modern learning. In Section II, the

[36] Dryden, "Translation of Virgil: Postscript to the Reader (1697)," in *Essays of John Dryden*, II, 240-42.

first chapter of the religious allegory, we are introduced to the three brothers as they distorted and later ignored the will of the father, as they defaced the cloaks of original Christianity under the influence of fashion, when simple and sufficient cloaks were no longer fashionable.[37] To establish the rationale of this change in fashion, Swift created sartorism, a system which displaced the father's influence by the influence of a tailor-deity.[38] Similarly, in the "Digression Concerning Criticks" Swift substitutes for the true critic the fashionable, Modern critic, exponent of the debased Modern learning.

Section IV and Section V, "A Digression in the Modern Kind"

The bridge between Section IV of *A Tale of a Tub*, the allegory dealing with Peter, and Section V, "A Digression in the Modern Kind," is achieved through the parallelism in the portraits of Peter, and Swift the *"freshest Modern"* and mock protagonist of the "Digression." Both are dedicated to "Pride, Projects, and Knavery." Peter turns *"Projector and Virtuoso"*; he "conceived the strangest Imaginations in the World"; and he tells the most outrageous lies. Through these projects, chiefly scientific in their satiric delineation, and through his "Imaginations," chiefly occult, Swift impugns some of the chief doctrines and disciplines of the Catholic Church. And just as Peter has abandoned the will of the Father

[37] See: Chap. 2, Sect. II, *supra*.
[38] See: Phillips, *op. cit.*, pp. 229, 230.

Dr. Phillips points out that several parts of Section II of the *Tale* are parody of Bentley, which would, it appears to me, indicate an even closer parallelism between the tailor-deity of Section II and the tailor-critic of Section III in the *Tale*. The fringe "which does also signify a broomstick" is obvious parody of Bentley, and Wotton noticed it in the third edition of his *Reflections*. The *"Calendae"* which was "sometimes writ with a *K*, but erroneously, for in best Copies it is ever spelt with a *C*" (p. 84), and the Ancient heritage of sartorism (p. 76) are parodies on Bentley's philological disquisitions, and on his learned descriptions of Ancient customs.

for something new and strange, so the protagonist of the "Digression in the Modern Kind" has abandoned his pure and Ancient heritage of learning. He finds Homer tolerable for an Ancient, but highly deficient in Modern accomplishments, i.e. chiefly scientific and occult accomplishments. Peter's projects form the basis and development of his holy, universal church; the protagonist of the "Digression" offers his highly alchemical formula to help his fellow Moderns achieve a universal system of all things known, believed, or imagined. Just as Peter's imaginations delude him into thinking himself superior to his father, so the Moderns' imaginations lead them to believe themselves superior to the Ancients. And just as Peter tells downright lies, so do the Moderns as delineated in the "Digression," in their prefaces and digressions, where they protest their imaginary greatness. Indeed, Dryden, whom Swift satirizes again in the "Digression in the Modern Kind," appears to be a very Lord Peter in learning.

Section VI *and Section* VII, "A Digression in Praise of Digressions"

In Section VI Swift presents the reformation of Martin and Jack, the period immediately after they escaped the domination of Lord Peter. In this section alone does Martin, the satiric norm, come to life; he is presented as a type of moderation and sweet reasonableness as he divests his cloak of the ornaments he was persuaded to add by Peter. In contrast, Jack is all tearing, flaying zeal. The principal theme connected with Jack in *A Tale of a Tub*, his madness, is barely introduced at the end of this section. Had Jack never gone farther in his zeal than tearing his coat to rid himself of Peter's influence, Swift would still have disliked him, but not with as much vigor as he does when Jack substitutes for Peter's projects and knavery his own madness. Undoubtedly Swift dis-liked Jack more than Peter, inasmuch as the Jacks were a considerably more palpable menace than the Peters when Swift wrote *A Tale of a Tub*. At this point, however, in Section VI, insofar as Jack as well as Martin are digressions from Peter, they earn Swift's praise.

"A Digression in Praise of Digressions" may be divided into two parts, of which the first part, devoted to a satire on that Modern refinement, the digression, is but an introduction to the second part, an angry condemnation of Modern learning as digressive from Ancient learning. Continuing the theme of Homer introduced into the previous digression, "A Digression in the Modern Kind," Swift characterizes a digression as a *"Nut-shell* in a[n] *Iliad"*;[39] and he indicates that a taste for digressions indicates a "Corruption and De-generacy of Taste," a *"debauched Appetite,"* and a *"crazy Constitution."* And Modern learning is a digression and a depredation; it is derived from titles and indices; Moderns become *"Scholars* and *Wits,* without the Fatigue of *Reading* or of *Thinking."* But Swift's severest condemnation of Modern learning is contained in his attack on the Modern scientific and pseudo-scientific systematization of learning, and between the two he makes no distinction. Thus:

. . . the Army of the Sciences hath been of late, with a World of Martial Discipline, drawn into its *close Order,* so that a View, or a Muster may be taken of it with abundance of Expedition. For this great Blessing we are wholly indebted to *Systems* and *Abstracts,* in which the *Modern* Fathers of Learning, like prudent Usurers, spent their Sweat for the Ease of Us their Children.

[39] "I have sometimes *heard* of an *Iliad* in a *Nut-shell;* but it hath been my Fortune much oftner to have *seen* a *Nut-shell* in a[n] *Iliad."* (*A Tale of a Tub,* p. 143.)

See Cowley's ode "To the Royal Society" in Sprat, *op. cit.,* p. 3:
"She with much stranger Art than his who put
All th' Iliads in a Nut,
The numerous works of Life does into Atomes shut."

Thus is Modernity rescued from "inglorious and undistin-
guisht Oblivion." Therefore one need read only critics and
commentators. Thus great Moderns will arise.

Swift concludes his "Digression in Praise of Digressions"
helpfully.

The Necessity of this Digression, will easily excuse the Length;
and I have chosen for it as proper a Place as I could readily find.
If the judicious Reader can assign a fitter, I do here empower
him to remove it into any other Corner he pleases.

At the same time that the "judicious reader" may not be
able to suggest a fitter corner, he must recognize that the
unity between the "Digression in Praise of Digressions" and
Section VI of the allegory is by no means as patent as the
unity between any other section of allegory and a digression
forming a unit in *A Tale of a Tub*. Perhaps Swift himself,
recognizing the weakness of his link, was moved to apologize
for the corner he chose for the "Digression in Praise of Digressions." The link, nevertheless, however weak, is there: Swift's
satirical praise of the Modern learning, a "reformation" of
the Ancient, and his half-hearted praise of the reformation
in religion, since the Reformation begot Nonconformity as
well as Establishment.

Section VIII *and* Section IX, "A Digression on Madness"

We have already traced in detail the relationship between
Aeolism of Section VIII of *A Tale of a Tub,* and Section IX,
"A Digression on Madness," establishing the mad, philosophic
state founded on vapor.[40] This unit is the most effective and
persuasive in *A Tale of a Tub;* it marks the climax of the
book, and it establishes the essential unity of Modern excesses

[40] See: Chap. 2, Sects. I and II, *supra.*

in religion and learning; both are reduced to absurdity and madness.

Section XI and Section X, Sometimes called "A Farther Digression"

In this unit the usual order is reversed so that the digression (called variously, "A Farther Digression," and "Compliments of the Author to the Reader," but more generally and least appropriately merely Section x), precedes the allegory, Section XI. The only plausible reason for this reversal is that Swift may have wished to conclude his religious allegory (as he does in Section XI) immediately before ending his whole book in "The Conclusion" which follows immediately after Section XI.[41]

In Section XI Swift follows the fortunes of Jack in very much the same way that he follows the fortunes of Peter in Section IV. Indeed, Jack and Peter are very closely identified in Section XI; they were frequently mistaken for one another, and eventually they joined forces against Martin, who, however, escaped them. But whereas Peter in A Tale of a Tub is conceived primarily as a scientific projector, as if all Catholicism were an elaborate project, Jack in Section XI, is conceived as a virtuoso in things of the spirit, as if to say that dissent was all spirit and no matter. Whereas Peter is full of "Pride, Projects, and Knavery," Jack is all zeal, madness and Enthusiasm in religion. The "Revolution of his Brain" led him into "a new and strange Variety of Conceptions, the Fruitfulness of his Imagination led him into certain Notions which, altho' in appearance very unaccountable, were not without their Mysteries and their Mean-

[41] In the first three editions of the Tale the Conclusion does not start a separate section, but is separated from Section XI by a line drawn across the middle of the page; the running title is merely A Tale of a Tub.

ings. . . ." Swift therefore recommends Jack's spiritual
vagaries to those:

. . . whose converting Imaginations dispose them to reduce all
Things into *Types*; who can make *Shadows*, no thanks to the Sun;
and then mold them into Substances, no thanks to Philosophy;
whose peculiar talent lies in fixing Tropes and Allegories to the
Letter, and refining what is Literal into Figure and Mystery.

In religion this obsession with the spiritual manifests itself
in dissent; in learning in occultism. The "Farther Digression,"
Swift's final and satirical burst of Modern self-gratification
and self-explication, ends with an extremely occult key "that
may be of great Assistance to those sublime Spirits, who shall
be appointed to labor in a universal Comment upon this
wonderful Discourse." He has already informed his readers
that he is exhausting all his talents in this discourse "for
the peculiar Advantage" of his "dear Country, and for the
universal Benefit of Mankind." He has provided for all his
readers, "the *Superficial*, the *Ignorant*, and the *Learned*."
As a dark author he offers innuendos to help others decipher
his work, "For *Night* being the universal Mother of Things,
wise Philosophers hold all Writings to be *fruitful* in Proportion they are *dark*." It is upon this occasion that he asks:

. . . that every prince in *Christendom* will take seven of the *deepest
Scholars* in his Dominions, and shut them up close for *seven* Years,
in *seven* Chambers, with a Command to write *seven* ample Commentaries on this comprehensive Discourse.

This burst of civilities was preceded, by way of introduction,
by Swift's satire on the Modern civilities between writer and
bookseller, writer and reader, and with a little digression
on the accidents to which the world is indebted to Modern
authors for their works. The bridge between Sections XI and
X of *A Tale of a Tub* lies between the spiritual lunacies of
Jack and the occult lunacies of Modern learning as it is
couched in writings of an essentially lunatic formlessness

and lack of matter. There is no matter in either the new learning or the new religion; all is of a deep, dark, and mysterious spirit.

"The Conclusion"

As a conclusion to a book which contains the systems of sartorism and Aeolism, the "Digression on Madness" and the "Digression Concerning Criticks," "The Conclusion" to *A Tale of a Tub* is unquestionably anticlimactic; it is, however, a deliberate anticlimax in parody of Modern conclusions, Swift's final parody on the Modern's lack of structure, method and substance.

I am now trying an Experiment very frequent among Modern Authors; which is, *to write upon Nothing*; when the Subject is utterly exhausted, to let the Pen still move on. . . .

A powerful conclusion to *A Tale of a Tub* might have been more satisfying in itself, but it would have broken the unity of effect implicit in the whole parody of Swift's structure of *A Tale of a Tub*. And philosophically, Swift's conclusion strikes exactly the right note, the tone of scepticism and pessimism which underlies *A Tale of a Tub* even in its most lighthearted and positive moments. For to Swift, the pessimist and moralist, what, indeed, had been concluded that he should conclude? Modernity marches on. Farewell.

[*The Mechanical Operation of the Spirit*

This so-called "fragment" (for it is actually a complete pamphlet of the "letter to a friend" variety) has, from the very first been printed along with *A Tale of a Tub* and *The Battle of the Books*, sometimes preceding both those works, sometimes following them. The relationship of *The Mechanical Operation of the Spirit* to the *Tale* and to the *Battle* has always been puzzling. To read *The Mechanical Operation*

A TALE OF A TUB

| *Satire on abuses in religion* | *Satire on abuses in learning* |

PREFATORY MATERIALS

"Treatises wrote by the same Author"

"An apology For the, &c"

"To The Right Honourable, John Lord Sommers"

"The Bookseller To The Reader"

"The Epistle Dedicatory, to His Royal Highness Prince Posterity"

"The Preface"

MAIN TEXT
Section i
"The Introduction"

Section ii The three brothers	Section iii "A Digression concerning Critics"
Section iv Peter	Section v "A Digression in the Modern Kind"
Section vi Martin and Jack	Section vii "A Digression in Praise of Digressions"

Section viii—Section ix
Aeolism   "A Digression on Madness"

Section xi Jack	Section x Sometimes called "A Farther Digression"

Section xii
"The Conclusion"

as the real conclusion to *A Tale of a Tub*, as opposed to the futile "Conclusion," is very probably a mistake.

Swift himself repudiated *The Mechanical Operation* as a casual sketch, not intended for publication, which he sent to a friend engaged in a similar work. That "friend," then, must have been engaged in another *Tale*. We have suggested that *The Battle of the Books* be read as a chapter of *A Tale of a Tub*; we suggest that *The Mechanical Operation* be read either as an early version of certain parts of *A Tale of a Tub*, or, more likely, as a portion of "*An Analytical Discourse upon Zeal*, Histori-theo-physi-logically *considered*," one of the "Treatises wrote by the same Author. . . which will be speedily published."[42] There is very little in *The Mechanical Operation* that is not done more fully and brilliantly in *A Tale of a Tub*; every theme in *The Mechanical Operation* is present in the *Tale*, and the satiric technique by which these themes are handled is much more sophisticated and subtle than the way in which they are developed in *The Mechanical Operation of the Spirit*.]

III

THE SATIRIC EFFECT

Every major point in *A Tale of a Tub*, a satire on the abuses in religion and learning, is made at least twice. In the prefatory apparatus coming before the "Preface" (and excluding the advertisement) the author speaks twice and the bookseller twice; each pens his own dedication. The "Preface" is balanced by another preface tucked away in the "Digression in the Modern Kind." The footnotes are balanced by the marginal notes. The general "Introduction" is balanced by

[42] Davis, ed., *A Tale of a Tub*, p. xxvii.

the introduction to the religious allegory in Section ii. The general "Conclusion" is balanced by the conclusion to the religious allegory in Section xi. But the pervasive symmetry and balance is handled with the greatest virtuosity in the body of *A Tale of a Tub,* in the five units each consisting of a section of the allegory and a digression. To see only the unity of all the digressions, and the unity of all the allegory, to find only a vertical order in *A Tale of a Tub* is to break it in half, to miss the essential symmetry; for a vertical order explains only the sequence of the sections of allegory and offers no explanation for the sequence of the digressions except that they are fortuitous.

The order of *A Tale of a Tub* is a horizontal order. Between the two members of each of the five units of allegory and digression there is, as we have tried to show, a common theme, an error, or aspect of an error common to religion and learning both. Sometimes this common theme within a unit of allegory and digression is developed comprehensively and in great detail, as in the unit composed of Aeolism and the "Digression on Madness." Sometimes the connection between the two members of a unit is very loose, so that although the main theme is introduced in each member, other themes take the foreground on occasion, as in the unit consisting of Section vi of the allegory and the "Digression in Praise of Digressions." Or, more simply, in some units the identification between allegory and digression is more complete and effective than in others. Nevertheless, whether the identification be complete or not, the order of the digressions is scarcely fortuitous; it is dependent upon the order of the allegory, which, in turn, is fixed chronologically by the narrative sequence of Swift's tale.

The position of one unit, however, that composed of Sections xi and x, is scarcely inevitable. One may well wonder why Swift did not reverse the order of his last two units in

A Tale of a Tub, so that Sections XI and X would come before Sections VIII and IX, and so that before its deliberately anti-climactic Conclusion, *A Tale of a Tub* might have risen to its climax in its most powerful unit, Aeolism and the "Digression on Madness." Such an arrangement, indeed, would have improved the vertical sequence of the allegory, for between Sections VI and XI of the allegory, dealing with Martin's and Jack's reformation, and with Jack's vagaries, respectively, there is the interruption to the narrative in Section VIII, Aeolism. And since the interest in Section VIII lies not so much in Jack as in the system he founded, since Swift's satire on occultism here is at least as important as the zeal which it discredits, Section VIII has much more of the tone of the digressions in *A Tale of a Tub* than of the allegory. And had Section VIII stood as the last of the allegorical sections, directly before the Conclusion, the break in tone would not have been so obvious. Whether a deliberate attempt at confusion and anticlimax was intended in this curious arrangement of the last two units of *A Tale of a Tub,* or whether here, at least, the arrangement was fortuitous must remain an open question.

There is no question, however, about the form of the individual sections of the allegory; they are merely chapters in a narrative. But what is the form of the individual digressions? By definition they have no form; they are composed of a series of little themes, sometimes only fragments of themes, each recalling some kind or aspect of the abuses in Modern learning, and the themes are combined and recombined in a variety of ways. Most of the digressions have very little unity and coherence. Remove them from *A Tale of a Tub,* take away the prop of the context, and they will not stand up alone as independent little essays. But this is just as it should be. A digression in parody of digressions necessitates a digressive formlessness. Swift's skill lay in his parody of formlessness at the same time that he achieved enough unity and coherence within his digressions to make his satire and parody inescapable, and to achieve a bridge between each digression and its parallel section of allegory. By and large it must be granted that Swift achieved all this, but with varying success upon different occasions, with the greatest success in "A Digression Concerning Criticks" and "A Digression on Madness," with considerably less skill in "A Digression in Praise of Digressions."

One might also question why Swift developed his satire on the abuses in learning in *A Tale of a Tub* in this devious and complicated way, why just as he devoted one chapter to the three brothers, one to Peter, one to Jack, etc., he did not devote one digression to a satire on science, another to philosophy, another to Grub Street, instead of intermingling the themes in all the digressions, in the prefatory apparatus, and even in the religious allegory. But once this question is asked, eventually one must ask why, indeed, Swift did not write two books, one satirizing the abuses in religion, and the other satirizing the abuses in learning. What Swift deplored in Modern religion and learning was not so much each individual abuse, nor even several abuses together, but the way in which and the extent to which all the abuses in religion and learning pervaded contemporary life and threatened the *status quo*. The abuses in religion and learning were interdependent and mutually inclusive. They formed the warp and woof of Modernity. They constituted Progress.

We can but marvel at the tremendous erudition and skill that Swift summoned in the *Tale* to shake his readers' faith in this Modern Progress, even as we recognize that in the literary history of civilization *A Tale of a Tub* represents a meaningful and prodigiously skillful espousal of a lost cause.

BIBLIOGRAPHY

Allbutt, Sir T. Clifford. *Greek Medicine in Rome*. London, Macmillan, 1921.

Allen, Robert J. *Clubs of Augustan London*. Cambridge, Harvard University Press, 1933 (*Harvard Studies in English*).

Aristophanes. *Plays*, ed. and trans., Benjamin Bickley Rogers. London, 1924, 3 vols. (*Loeb Classical Library*).

Aristotle. *Organon, or Logical Treatises, with the Introduction of Porphyry*, ed. and trans., Octavius Freire Owen. London, 1853, 2 vols. (*Bohn Classical Library*).

Aristotle. *Problems*, ed. and trans., W. S. Hett. New York, 1936-1937, 2 vols. (*Loeb Classical Library*).

Arnauld, Antoine and Nicole, Pierre. *Port Royal Logic (Art of Thinking)*, ed. and trans., Thomas Spencer Baynes. London, Wm. Blackwood and Sons, 1872, 10th ed.

Athenian Society. *Athenian Gazette: or Casuistical Mercury, Resolving all the most Nice and Curious Questions Proposed by the Ingenious*. London, printed for John Dunton, 1691-1697, 20 vols.

Athenian Society. *Athenian Oracle. Being an Entire Collection of all the Valuable Questions and Answers in the Old Athenian Mercuries*. London, 1728, 4 vols., 3rd ed. Vol. IV contains Charles Gildon's *History of the Athenian Society*.

Athenian Society. *Young-Students-Library, Containing Extracts and Abridgments of the Most Valuable Books Printed in England, and in the Forreign Journals, From the Year Sixty Five, to this Time*. London, printed for John Dunton, 1691.

Atterbury, Francis. *Short Review of the Controversy between Mr. Boyle, and Dr. Bentley*. London, printed for A. Baldwin, 1701.

Bacon, Sir Francis. *Philosophical Works of Francis Bacon*, ed., John M. Robertson, from the texts and translations of Ellis and Spedding. New York, E. P. Dutton, 1905.

Bailey, Cyril. *Greek Atomists and Epicurus*. Oxford, Clarendon Press, 1928.

Baldwin, James Mark, ed. *Dictionary of Philosophy and Psychology*. New York, Macmillan, 1905-1911, 3 vols.

Beattie, Lester, M. *John Arbuthnot, Mathematician and Satirist.* Cambridge, Harvard University Press, 1935 (*Harvard Studies in English.*)

Bentley, Richard. *Works of Richard Bentley,* ed., Alexander Dyce. London, Francis Macpherson, 1836, 3 vols.

Berwick, Donald M. *Reputation of Jonathan Swift (1781-1882).* Philadelphia, 1941.

Blackmore, Sir Richard. *Essays upon Several Subjects.* London, printed for E. Curll, 1716.

Blackmore, Sir Richard. *Prince Arthur.* London, printed for Awnsham and Churchill, 1696, 3rd ed. corrected.

Boyce, Benjamin. *Tom Brown of Facetious Memory.* Cambridge, Harvard University Press, 1939 (*Harvard Studies in English*).

Boyle, Charles (4th Earl of Cork and Orerry). *Dr. Bentley's Dissertations on the Epistles of Phalaris, and the Fables of Aesop, Examin'd.* London, printed for Tho. Bennet, 1698.

———. Φαλαριδος Ακραγαντινων Τυραννοι Επιστολαι, *Phalaridis Agrigentinorum Tyranni Epistolae.* Oxford, Clarendon Press, 1718.

Boyle, Robert. *Christian Virtuoso.* London, printed for John Taylor, 1690.

———. *Occasional Reflections Upon Several Subjects.* London, printed for Henry Herringman, 1665.

———. *Some Considerations Touching the Usefulnesse of Experimental Natural Philosophy.* Oxford, printed for R. Davis, 1664-1671, 2d ed.

———. *Some Physico-Theological Considerations about the Possibility of Resurrection.* London, printed for H. Herringman, 1675.

Bredvold, Louis I. "Dryden, Hobbes, and the Royal Society," *Modern Philology,* xxv, 417-38 (May 1928).

———. *Intellectual Milieu of John Dryden.* Ann Arbor, Michigan, University of Michigan Press, 1934 (*University of Michigan Publications*).

Browne, Sir Thomas. *Works of Sir Thomas Browne,* ed., Charles Sayle. Edinburgh, John Grant, 1912, 3 vols.

Buck, Albert H. *Growth of Medicine from the Earliest Times to about 1800.* New Haven, Yale University Press, 1917.

Burlingame, Anne Elizabeth. *Battle of the Books in its Historical Setting.* New York, B. W. Huebsch, 1920.

Burton, Robert. *Anatomy of Melancholy*. New York, Empire State Book Co., 1924.

Bury, J. B. *Idea of Progress*. London, Macmillan, 1920.

Butler, Samuel. *Genuine Remains in Verse and Prose of Mr. Samuel Butler*, ed., R. Thayer. London, Tonson, 1759, 2 vols.

————. *Poetical Works of Samuel Butler*, ed., Reginald Brimley Johnson. London, George Bell and Sons, 1893, 2 vols.

Campbell, Lily B. *Shakespeare's Tragic Heroes, Slaves of Passion*. Cambridge, Cambridge University Press, 1930.

Campbell, Oscar James. *Comicall Satyre and Shakespeare's Troilus and Cressida*. San Marino, California, 1938 (*Huntington Library Publications*).

Casaubon, Meric. *Treatise Concerning Enthusiasme*. London, printed for Roger Daniel, 1656, 2d ed. rev.

Croll, Morris W. "Baroque Style in Prose," *Studies in English Philology in Honor of Frederick Klaeber*, eds., Kemp Malone and Martin B. Ruud. Minneapolis, University of Minnesota Press, 1929.

Davis, Herbert. *Satire of Jonathan Swift*. New York, Macmillan, 1947.

Dennis, John. *Original Letters, Familiar, Moral, and Critical*. London, Wm. Mears, 1721, 2 vols. in one.

Descartes, Rene. *Descartes Selections*, ed., Ralph M. Eaton. New York, Scribner's Sons, 1927 (*Modern Students' Library, Philosophy Series*).

Dictionary of National Biography.

D'Israeli, Isaac. *Quarrels of Authors*. London, printed for John Murray, 1814, 3 vols.

Dryden, John. *Essays of John Dryden*, ed., W. P. Ker. Oxford, Clarendon Press, 1926, 2 vols.

Duncan, C. S. "Scientist as a Comic Type," *Modern Philology*, XIV, 281-91 (Sept. 1916).

————. *New Science and English Literature in the Classical Period*. Menasha, Wisconsin, Collegiate Press, 1913.

Dunton, John. *Life and Errors of John Dunton*. London, printed for S. Malthus, 1705.

Encyclopedia Britannica (14th ed.).

Fontenelle, Bernard le Bouvier de. *Oeuvres de Monsieur de Fontenelle*. Amsterdam, Francois Chaugnion, 1764, 12 vols.

Foster, Sir Michael. *Lectures on the History of Physiology during the 16th, 17th, and 18th Centuries*. Cambridge, Cambridge University Press, 1924.

Garrison, Fielding H. *Introduction to the History of Medicine*, Philadelphia, W. B. Saunders, 1922, 3rd ed. rev.

Gildon, Charles. *History of the Athenian Society*. See Athenian Society, *Athenian Oracle*.

Gillot, Hubert. *La Querelle des Anciens et des Modernes en France*. Paris, Honore Champion, 1914 (*Librairie Ancienne*).

Glanvil, Joseph. *Vanity of Dogmatizing*. New York, Facsimile Text Society, 1931.

Gordon, Thomas (?). *Dedication to a Great Man, Concerning Dedications*. London, printed for James Roberts, 1718, 3rd ed.

Graham, Elsie C. *Optics and Vision*. New York, 1929.

Green, J. R. *Short History of the English People*. New York, Harper and Brothers, 1876, 2 vols. (*Everyman's Library*).

Grew, Nehemiah. *Musaeum Regalis Societatis*. London, printed by W. Rawlins, 1681.

Guthkelch, A., ed. *Battle of the Books by Jonathan Swift; with Selections from the Literature of the Phalaris Controversy*. London, Chatto and Windus, 1908 (*King's Classics*).

Guthkelch, A. C. and D. Nichol Smith, eds. *Tale of a Tub to which is added The Battle of the Books and the Mechanical Operation of the Spirit. By Jonathan Swift*. Oxford, Clarendon Press, 1920.

H., W. *Puritan Convert*. London, 1676.

Haller, William. *Rise of Puritanism*. New York, Columbia University Press, 1938.

Harsh, Philip Whaley. *Handbook of Classical Drama*. Stanford, California, Stanford University Press, 1944.

Hatfield, Theodore M. "John Dunton's Periodicals," *Journalism Quarterly*, x, 209-25 (Sept. 1933).

Hobbes, Thomas. *Leviathan.* New York, Harpers, 1937 (*Everyman's Library*).

Hopkins, Arthur John. *Alchemy, Child of Greek Philosophy.* New York, Columbia University Press, 1934.

Houghton, Walter E. Jr. "English Virtuoso in the Seventeenth Century," *Journal of the History of Ideas*, Part I, III, 51-73; Part II, III, 190-219 (Jan., April 1942).

Jebb, R. C. "Aristophanes," *Encyclopedia Britannica* (14th ed.).
———. *Bentley.* New York, Macmillan 1889 (*English Men of Letters*).

Johnson, Samuel. "Swift," *Lives of the English Poets*, ed., George Birckbeck Hill, Oxford, Clarendon Press, 1905, 3 vols.

Jones, Richard Foster. *Ancients and Moderns.* St. Louis, Missouri, 1936 (*Washington University Studies*).
———. "Background of the *Battle of the Books*," *Washington University Studies*, VII, No. 2, 99-162 (April 1920).

Kerby-Miller, Charles, ed. *Memoirs of the Extraordinary Life, Works, and Discoveries of Martinus Scriblerus,* by Pope, Swift, Gay, etc., New Haven, Conn., Yale University Press, 1950.

King, William. *Original Works of William King.* London, 1776, 3 vols.

Kligman, Elsie. *Contemporary Opinion of Swift,* 1932. (An unpublished Columbia University Master's Essay.)

Krapp, Robert M. "Wit and Sense in Seventeenth Century English Literature," *Science and Society*, X, 80-92 (Winter 1946).

Landa, Louis A. and James Edward Tobin, *Jonathan Swift, A List of Critical Studies Published from 1895 to 1945.* New York, 1945 (*Eighteenth Century Bibliographical Pamphlets*).

Lord, Louis E. *Aristophanes, His Plays and His Influence.* New York, Longmans Green, 1927 (*Our Debt to Greece and Rome*).

Lovejoy, Arthur O. " 'Pride' in Eighteenth-Century Thought," *Modern Language Notes*, XXXVI, 31-37 (Jan. 1921).
———. *Great Chain of Being.* Cambridge, Harvard University Press, 1942.

Lucretius. *De Rerum Natura,* ed. and trans., W. H. D. Rouse. London, 1928 (*Loeb Classical Library*).

Macdonald, Hugh. *John Dryden, A Bibliography of Early Editions and of Drydeniana.* Oxford, Clarendon Press, 1939.

Marburg, Clara. *Sir William Temple, A Seventeenth Century "Libertin."* New Haven, Yale University Press, 1932.

Marlborough, Sarah, Duchess of. *Memoirs of Sarah, Duchess of Marlborough,* ed., William King. London, George Routledge and Sons, 1930.

Maynwaring, Arthur. *Life and Posthumous Works of Arthur Maynwaring.* London, printed for A. Bell, 1715.

Mayo, Thomas Franklin. *Epicurus in England (1650-1725).* Texas, Southwest Press, 1934.

Merton, Robert K. "Puritanism, Pietism, and Science," *Sociological Review,* XXVIII, 1-30 (Jan. 1936).

Milton, John. *Student's Milton,* ed., Frank Allen Patterson. New York, Appleton-Century-Crofts, Inc., 1936, rev. ed.

More, Louis Trenchard. *Life and Works of the Honourable Robert Boyle.* New York, Oxford University Press, 1944.

Murray, Gilbert. *Aristophanes.* New York, Oxford University Press, 1933.

Nicolson, Marjorie Hope, ed. *Conway Letters.* New Haven, Yale University Press, 1930.

Oxford English Dictionary.

Phillips, Mabel (Mrs. Clyde de Vane). *Jonathan Swift's Relation to Science,* 1925. (An unpublished Yale University doctoral dissertation.)

Pons, Emile. *Swift: Les Années de Jeunesse et le "Conte du Tonneau."* London, Oxford University Press, 1925.

Pope, Alexander. *Works of Alexander Pope,* ed., William Lisle Bowles. London, 1806, 10 vols.

Price, Rebecca. *Studies in Thomas Vaughan,* 1942. (An unpublished Columbia University Master's Essay.)

Quintana, Ricardo. *Mind and Art of Jonathan Swift.* New York, Oxford University Press, 1936.

Ray, John. *Three Physico-Theological Discourses.* London, printed for William Innys, 1713, 3rd ed.

Read, John. *Prelude to Chemistry.* London, George Bell and Sons, 1936.

Redinger, Ruby V. "Jonathan Swift, the Disenchanter," *American Scholar,* XV, 221-26 (1946).

Rigault, H. *Histoire de la Querelle des Anciens et des Modernes,* Paris, Hachette, 1856.

Royal Society of London, *Philosophical Transactions of the Royal Society of London,* 1665-1700. (No transactions were published between 1679-1682.)

Shadwell, Thomas. *Virtuoso.* London, printed for Henry Herringman, 1676.

Sheridan, Thomas. *Life of the Rev. Dr. Jonathan Swift.* London, 1787, 2d ed.

Spingarn, Joel E., ed. *Critical Essays of the Seventeenth Century.* Oxford, Clarendon Press, 1908-1909, 3 vols.

Sprat, Thomas. *History of the Royal-Society of London,* 1702, 2d ed. corrected.

Steeves, Harrison Ross. " 'Athenian Virtuosi' and 'Athenian Society,' " *Modern Language Review,* VII, 358-71 (July 1912).

———. *Learned Societies and English Literary Scholarship.* New York, Columbia University Press, 1913.

Stubbe, Henry. *Campanella Revived, or an Enquiry into the History of the Royal Society.* London, 1670.

Swift, Jonathan. *Correspondence of Jonathan Swift,* ed., F. Elrington Ball. London, G. Bell and Sons, 1910-1914, 6 vols.

———. *Prose Works of Jonathan Swift,* ed., Temple Scott. London, George Bell, 1898-1908, 12 vols. (*Bohn's Standard Library*).

———. *Prose Works of Jonathan Swift,* ed., Herbert Davis. Oxford, Basil Blackwell, vol. I (*A Tale of a Tub*), 1939, vol. XI (*Gulliver's Travels*), 1941.

———. *Works of Jonathan Swift,* eds., John Hawksworth, Abel Bowyer, Deane Swift, John Nichols. London, 1764-1775, 25 vols.

———. *Tale of a Tub to which is added The Battle of the Books and the Mechanical Operation of the Spirit,* eds., A. C.

Guthkelch and D. Nichol Smith. Oxford, Clarendon Press, 1920.
————. *Tale of a Tub*. New York, Columbia University Press, 1930. (With a Foreword by Edward Hodnett.)

Teerink, H. *Bibliography of the Writings in Prose and Verse of Jonathan Swift*, Hague, Martinus Nijhoff, 1937.
Temple, Sir William. *Works of Sir William Temple*. London, 1814, 4 vols.
Thorpe, Clarence DeWitt. *Aesthetic Theory of Thomas Hobbes*. Ann Arbor, Michigan, University of Michigan Press, 1940 (*University of Michigan Publications*).
Tillyard, E. M. W. *Elizabethan World Picture*. London, Chatto and Windus, 1943.

Vaughan, Thomas. *Magical Writings of Thomas Vaughan*, ed., Arthur Edward Waite. London, George Redway, 1888.
————. *Works of Thomas Vaughan; Eugenius Philalethes*, ed., Arthur Edward Waite. London, Theosophical Publishing House, 1919.

Waite, Arthur Edward. *Holy Kabbalah*. New York, Macmillan, 1928.
————. *Occult Sciences*. New York, E. P. Dutton, 1923. (Facsimile of the 1891 ed.)
Webster, C. M. "Puritans' Ears in *A Tale of a Tub*," *Modern Language Notes*, XLVII, 96-97 (Feb. 1932).
————. "Swift's *Tale of a Tub* Compared with Earlier Satires of the Puritans," *Publications of the Modern Language Association*, XLVII, 171-78 (March 1932).
Wedel, T. O. "On the Philosophical Background of *Gulliver's Travels*," *Studies in Philology*, XXIII, 434-50 (Oct. 1926).
Wiener, Philip P. "Leibniz's Project of a Public Exhibition of Scientific Inventions," *Journal of the History of Ideas*, I, 232-40 (April 1940).
Williams, Harold. *Dean Swift's Library*. Cambridge, Cambridge University Press, 1932.
Williamson, George. "Restoration Revolt against Enthusiasm," *Studies in Philology*, XXX, 571-603 (Oct. 1933).
Wilson, John. *Dramatic Works*, eds., J. Maidment and W. H.

Logan. Edinburgh, W. Peterson, 1874 (*Dramatists of the Restoration*).

Wing, Donald Godard. *Short-Title Catalogue of Books Printed in England. . . 1641-1700*. New York, Columbia University Press, 1945, vol. I. (I am indebted to the Columbia University Library for allowing me to examine the MS of the yet unpublished portions of this bibliography.)

Wolf, A. *History of Science, Technology, and Philosophy in the 16th and 17th Centuries*. London, Allen and Unwin, 1935.

Woodbridge, Homer E. *Sir William Temple, The Man and his Work*. New York, Oxford University Press, 1940 (*Publication of the Modern Language Association*).

Wotton, William. *Defense of the Reflections Upon Ancient and Modern Learning*. London, printed for Tim. Goodwin, 1705.

———. *Reflections upon Ancient and Modern Learning.* London, printed by J. Leake, 1694.

———. *Reflections upon Ancient and Modern Learning.* London, printed by J. Leake, 1697, 2d ed.

Zilboorg, Gregory and George W. Henry. *History of Medical Psychology*. New York, W. W. Norton, 1941.

INDEX

Alcibiades, 125, 126
Allbutt, Sir T. Clifford, 27, 147
Allen, Robert J., 76, 147
Apollonius of Tyana, 32
Arbuthnot, John, 112
Aristophanes, 125-28, 147
Aristotle, 20, 25, 26, 35, 37, 49, 58, 59, 88, 127, 147
Aristoxenus, 31
Arnauld, Antoine and Pierre Nicole, 58, 59, 147
Artephius, 55
Athenian Society, 79-84, 149
Atterbury, Francis, 16-19, 93, 94, 99, 147

Bacon, Sir Francis, 5, 9-11, 20, 21, 37, 47, 64-69, 71, 77, 82, 90, 96, 147
Bailey, Cyril, 31, 39, 147
Baldwin, James Mark, 27, 147
Beattie, Lester M., 112, 148
Bentley, Richard, 16-19, 51, 85, 93-104, 108, 109, 117, 135, 148
Berwick, Donald, xiii, 148
Blackmore, Sir Richard, xi, xii, 108, 118, 119, 148
Boccaccio, 116
Boccalini, 116
Bodin, Jean, 90
Boehme (Behmen), Jacob, 49, 54, 55, 91
Bolton, Edmund, 77
Boyce, Benjamin, 80, 83, 148
Boyle, Charles, 16-19, 93-96, 103, 148
Boyle, Robert, 19, 65, 66, 70, 72, 74, 110, 119, 148
Bredvold, Louis I., 11, 33, 108, 148
Brown, Tom, 80, 108
Browne, Peter, xi, xii
Browne, Sir Thomas, 32, 48, 119, 148
Buck, Albert H., 26, 148
Burlingame, Anne Elizabeth, xiv, 148

Burton, Robert, 28, 107, 149
Bury, J. B., 4, 6, 67, 68, 90, 149
Butler, Samuel, 25, 47, 51-55, 149

Campanella, 90
Campbell, Lily B., 28, 36, 149
Campbell, Oscar James, 127, 149
Cardan, 90
Casaubon, Meric, 15, 23, 39, 51, 149
Cervantes, 116
Christ Church Wits, 18, 95, 97, 98
Cicero, 119
Cleon, 125-27
Clifford, James, 109
Comenius, 77
Cowley, Abraham, 77, 137
Croll, Morris W., 119, 149
Ctesias, 102

Davis, Herbert, xiii, 5, 8, 129, 143, 149
De la Croze, Jean Cornado, 82
Demosthenes, 125
Dennis, John, xi, xii, 100, 108, 117, 119, 149
Descartes, René, 5, 8, 10, 11, 13, 20, 21, 26, 29-34, 58, 67, 68, 71, 149
Diodorus, 102, 103
Diogenes, 33
D'Israeli, Isaac, 73, 149
Dorset, Earl of, 114, 115
Dryden, John, 11, 34, 40, 77, 108, 109, 113-17, 119, 121, 122, 129, 133-36, 149
Duncan, C. S., 70, 71, 76, 149
Dunton, John, 79-84, 149
D'Urfey, Thomas, 92, 108, 109, 117

Epicurus, xv, 15, 20, 21, 25, 30-44, 50, 51, 56, 62, 88
Erasmus, 128
Evelyn, John, 77

Farnaby, Thomas, 99
Fontenelle, Bernard, 88, 90, 150
Foster, Sir Michael, 26, 27, 29, 150